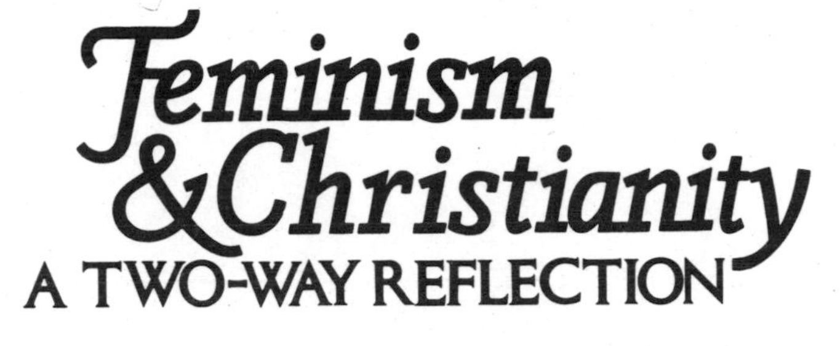
Feminism
&Christianity
A TWO-WAY REFLECTION

Other books by Denise Lardner Carmody:

Women and World Religion Abingdon
The Oldest God Abingdon
*Contemporary Catholic Theology: An Introduction** Harper & Row
*Ways to the Center: An Introduction to World Religions** Wadsworth
*Christianity: An Introduction** Wadsworth
What Are They Saying About Non-Christian Faith? Paulist

*with John Tully Carmody

Feminism & Christianity

A TWO-WAY REFLECTION

DENISE LARDNER CARMODY

ABINGDON / NASHVILLE

FEMINISM AND CHRISTIANITY: A TWO-WAY REFLECTION

Library of Congress Cataloging in Publication Data

CARMODY, DENISE LARDNER, 1935-
Feminism and Christianity.

Includes bibliographical references and index.
1. Woman (Christian theology) 2. Feminism—Religious aspects—Christianity. I. Title.
BT704.C37 261.8'344 82-1709 AACR2

ISBN 0-687-12914-1

MANUFACTURED BY THE PARTHENON PRESS AT
NASHVILLE, TENNESSEE, UNITED STATES OF AMERICA

For
Jessica Corlett (b. 1977)
and
Abigail Snyder (b. 1977)
in hopes that they find 2000 a very good year

CONTENTS

PREFACE

The main audience I have in mind for this book is the centrist group who see merit in both feminist and Christian claims. While few people are likely to agree with all the positions I take, most people who have not foreclosed the possibility of gaining wisdom from both raised feminist consciousness and the gospel will find some bones worth chewing.

The book is neither a full-scale report on recent literature in the feminist and Christian camps nor a full-scale original essay, but something midway between the two. This testifies to my perception of the current need, as well as to my failures of nerve.

I owe thanks to the various women's groups I have worked with in the School Sisters of Notre Dame, at Penn State University, and at Wichita State. My husband, John Carmody, supplied bibliographic help and stronger turns of phrase, while Karla Kraft of Wichita State's Religion Department typed the manuscript expertly. To them, too, my thanks.

INTRODUCTION: BEHIND THE TITLE

This book is an effort to reconcile and coordinate two allegiances. I first thought of it in confrontational terms: Feminism versus Christianity. On further reflection, however, I decided that this fashioned a false dichotomy, for in my bones I believe that good people of different nominal allegiances usually hold more in common than they hold apart. So, too, with the profound versions of superficially antagonistic philosophies or world-views. The wise person does not care about names, Aquinas opined. The person of deep honesty and love responds to other people of deep honesty and love, even when they "should" be her enemies, because "deep calls to deep." Let me try to illustrate this thesis concretely.

Karl Rahner, the prolific Roman Catholic theologian, has squarely faced the problems of deep interpretation, showing how his theory—that profound human beings of whatever stripe may be called "anonymous Christians"—works out in practice:

> I must assert as a Christian and a metaphysician who holds that the spiritual element in man cannot be reduced to matter that even a materialist philosopher does those free, spiritual activities which I objectify in a philosophy of spirit, even if the empiricist affirms that such activities do not in fact exist. A Marxist philosopher of history certainly interprets my role as a priest differently from the way I do. From a formal point of view, then, there is no problem in my treating someone as an anonymous Christian, even if he energetically denies my interpretation and

> rejects it as false or incoherent; Nishitani the well known Japanese philosopher, the head of the Kyoto school, who is familiar with the notion of the anonymous Christian, once asked me: What would you say to my treating you as an anonymous Zen Buddhist? I replied: certainly you may and should do so from your point of view: I feel myself honoured by such an interpretation, even if I am obliged to regard you as being in error or if I assume that, correctly understood, to be a genuine Zen Buddhist is identical with being a genuine Christian, in the sense directly and properly intended by such statements. Of course in terms of objective awareness it is indeed clear that the Buddhist is not a Christian and the Christian is not a Buddhist. Nishitani replied: Then on this point we are entirely at one.[1]

A first sketch of my orientation, then, is that it involves a suspicion that to be a genuine feminist is very like being a genuine Christian. "Genuine" obviously is the difficult word, and what I want it to connote will only become clear in the course of these reflections. But we live in a time when philosophers of science increasingly appreciate the ways that theory precedes and guides the study of data, a time in which philosophers of humanistic interpretation increasingly agree that a hermeneutical circle links the exegete's conclusions to her starting pre-judices. My starting theory and prejudice is that the quality of the players' game matters more than their uniforms. From the outset, I refuse to choose between my good friend of lesbian orientation, who shies away from organized religion because it calls her depraved, and my good friend of Christian orientation, who prays that Jesus will care for her wandering tribe of ten children. Radical lesbians and fundamentalist Christians can rant as they wish. A plague on both their houses, I say, for neither has much depth or compassion.

At the heart of Rahner's anonymous Christianity is a distinction between a person's unthematic or preconceptual knowledge and convictions and her knowledge and convictions that have been objectified in concepts and words. The person herself may not be fully aware of this difference, but it has enormous significance. There is a vast reservoir of what

Michael Polanyi calls "tacit" understanding that seldom, or perhaps even never, is expressly articulated. We always "know," in an intuitive, holistic way, more than we do (indeed, more than we can) realize and say. Both depth psychology and humanistic anthropology such as Rahner's appreciate the complexities, at times even the contradictions, that afflict the human "spirit-in-the-world."

As spirit, the person can return to herself, in reflective analysis and contemplative self-possession. As spirit, she has a measure of judgmental capacity, through which she can assert that the conditions for the existence of something have, or have not, been fulfilled. As spirit, she has a measure of freedom, of self-donation to a given one among a number of possible goods or choices of action, because none of them is completely compelling. As material, anchored in the world, the human person never can know herself to the essence. Her judgments seldom deal with pure cases, in which all the conditions have been fulfilled, and her freedom is seldom very exalted, or very far removed from compulsions and irrationalities.

As a result, there can be considerable discord between what a person believes or knows at heart and the way that she expresses herself. Add the tendency of social bodies to do business by slogans and checklists, and you have an immense field of people who are difficult really to assess. Thus the relevance of the biblical criterion for discernment: by their fruits you will know them. This is the second sketch of my orientation: I am more interested in fruits than in verbal claims. It is also the reason why my two women friends are actually sisters. So different in their overt, expressed allegiances, they are the same in their human fruitfulness. They are both honest and loving; they are both what I understand "humane" and "Christian" finally to denote.

CONCORDIA

Writers who enjoy their work usually like to play with words. I have been playing with notions that undercut many of the verbal oppositions between parties such as "feminists" and "Christians," trying to move toward the reasons of the heart, the area of con-cord. Therefore, I was amused to find a recent experience I had in Concordia, Kansas, dancing outside my storehouse of examples. Concordia is a small town in the north-central part of the state. I had bedded down there in Manna House, a place of prayer run by the Sisters of Saint Joseph, prior to speaking on "Women in the Church" to the sisters' biannual senate. Manna House was banked in quiet, as befits a place of prayer. But quiet, prayer, and sleep were not to be that night, for on weekends the streets around Manna House become a drag strip, where the boys of Concordia race their pickups. Having nothing better to do, and no love for the peace of their town, the boys burn their tires, blast their horns, and backfire their souped-up engines from dark to four in the morning. The whole scene struck me as an epitome of our current cultural stupidity, a perfect little specimen of the macho mechanism I would have feminism and Christianity conspire to wreck.

For money and madness, American culture now gives the kids of many towns nothing better for their glands and boredom than hard, bumping noise. A generation ago it gave hundreds of thousands of them nothing better than a tour of Vietnam, so I am not saying present days are the worst of times. I am saying the feminism and Christianity I revere are ways of life opposed to the spiritual deadliness of our current noise, mechanization, and martial stridency. I am saying that both these ways of life stand resolutely against the trivialization and destructiveness rampant in a culture that ignores the soul.

On the popular levels, this culture expresses itself in noise and acquisitiveness. It is all talk and things. On the middling, institutional levels, it shows itself as a thralldom to economics and putative power. Taxes and inflation dominate its boardrooms, because taxes and inflation diminish its great god, profit. Status and arms-building preoccupy its men of position, because its men of position assume that the military-industrial complex houses most people of account.

On the upper levels, the soullessness of our culture shows in the sterility of the university and the Church. So far as things of the deep spirit are concerned, the university has made a desert and called it peace. Superb at negative criticism, able to analyze every empirical defect and logical flaw, the university knows less about the tranquillity of order (Augustine's definition of real peace) than the humblest peasant apprenticed to the seasons. Nor is the Church much better. Neither intellectually nor politically has the American Church incarnated Irenaeus's conviction that God's glory is human beings fully alive. Not radically set for contemplation and justice, the Church has become a central part of the problem.

The antidote to this state of affairs is a genuine, passionate religion, whose core, as Bernard Lonergan has shown, is being in love without restriction.[2] Recently Wilfred Cantwell Smith has made the historical case for the rights of such a religion in our current situation, challenging the negative secularism that afflicts so many intellectuals:

> The striving to understand religion is part and parcel of, certainly not subordinate to, man's general aspiration to truth.
>
> Some among my Western readers might in this regard expect consideration to be given to the question of the truth of transcendence itself, the reality of God. One of the advantages of familiarity with the world history of religion (of man) is that one is then not intimidated by current Western trends of thought that see this as a "problem." Rather than feeling called upon to defend this awareness of what some of us call the divine before the bar of modern sceptics' particular logic and exceptional world-view, I am at least equally inclined to call them before the bar of world history to defend their curious insensitivity to this dimension of human life. Seen in global perspective, current anti-transcendent thinking is an aberration. Intellectuals are challenged, indeed, to understand it: how has it arisen that for the first time on this earth a significant group has failed to discern the larger context of being human, and has even tried (with results none too encouraging thus far) to modify its inherited civilisation so. After all, the overwhelming majority of intelligent

> persons at most times and places, and all cultures other than in part the recent West, have recognized the transcendent quality of man and the world. To be secularist in the negative sense is to be oddly parochial in both space and time, and to opt for what may alas be a dying culture. It is important that we keep in conversation with this group; but important also that we not fall victim to, nor treat with anything but compassion, its incapacity to see.[3]

I shall offer a few feminist comments on this quotation momentarily, but its gist should stand clear: by what superior fruits of wisdom, what more beautiful and more effective love, does current secularism propose to banish God?

THE AMBIGUITIES OF FEMINISM

The experience of transcendent mystery, of what much of the East calls the Buddhanature and much of the West calls God, detonates the secularist prison. Where secularism sees only two dimensions, a spiritual flatland, humanism or religion face to face with mystery sees a third dimension, a world of sacraments. Contrary to this passage from Smith, however, we must make it clear that the world history of religion shows that most men *and women* have opposed the current anti-transcendent thinking and would call it an aberration. Contrary to so many theologians' curious insensitivity to the sexual dimension of human language, we must make it clear that the larger context of being human today has also to recognize the transcendent quality of woman. Otherwise we will be oddly parochial in our religion and opt for what likely is an oppressive faith.

This combination of mystagogy and feminism goes down hard in many quarters. What I would call a centrist position, embracing both contemplative absorption in God and firm work for social justice, easily comes under fire from both the left and the right. From the secularist left, the attack fits the quotation from Smith. Thus I have found myself the target of antireligious feminists, who feel that religion can only be a bastion of oppression. For example, a reviewer of a manuscript for a women's studies text that women faculty at Penn State had produced[4] said that my chapter on religion was inappropriate—that religion had no place in such a textbook. Statistics, history, literature, and sociology all had a place, but any consideration of the ways that most women have ultimately construed the world was inappropriate. When Smith speaks of "an incapacity to see" no doubt he has this sort of blindness in mind. I would only underscore the arrogance with which the blindness often is allied.

A slightly different version of religious blindness or illiteracy raised its head recently during a panel discussion between a nationally prominent feminist and some local scholars. The prominent feminist had explained her return to many of the values of her Jewish parents, now that she has grandchildren. She had groped for the religious diction of her childhood, trying to remember what they called the group of Jews necessary for a prayer session *(minyan),* and how many men were its minimal number (ten). Clearly, Jewish theology did not rank high on this woman's list of competencies. Nonetheless, she turned on me with the dramatic outrage of the practiced performer when I suggested that many women condemned to endure unjust situations understandably take solace in religion. For this feminist, prayer and religious consolation can only represent alienation, and the bigger questions to which they lead (such as how to live with meaning *now,* in the days when the classless society manifestly has not come) are *verboten.*

One scarcely knows how to reply to this dazzling combination of ignorance and arrogance. As Voegelin has seen in the case of Marx, it represents a spiritual disease quite far advanced.[5] Because the admission of transcendence is unthinkable, reality shrinks to economics and politics: Be of good cheer, suffering women of the world, the meaninglessness of your lives doesn't matter. One day your daughters will be chewing cigars and swapping votes like any political son.

From the religious right, however, come outbursts of idiocy equally offensive. For example, the antifeminism of Jerry Falwell and Phyllis Schlafly conflates biblical fundamentalism with right-wing politics in ways that would embarrass a good cartoon. Thus Falwell on the Equal Rights Amendment: "ERA is not merely a political issue, but a moral issue as well. A definite violation of holy Scripture, ERA defies the mandate that 'the husband is the head of the wife, even as Christ is the head of the church' (Eph. 5:23). In I Peter 3:7 we read that husbands are to give their wives honor as unto the weaker vessel, that they are both heirs together of the grace of life. Because a woman is weaker does not mean she is less important."[6] This is from the man who thinks that the free-enterprise system is clearly outlined in the book of Proverbs,[7] and from the man who quotes the woman (Schlafly) who thinks that "another dogma of the women's liberationists is that you have no right to make a moral judgment between what is right and what is wrong."[8] Those in the know are therefore not expecting much intellectual wattage. Still, such right-wing stupidity makes all of Christianity liable to contempt.

In more subtle ways, conservative Christianity that fails to define terms and is overly solicitous of the faith of the weak alienates strong women of good will, who could be genuine allies. A reviewer of my *Women and World Religions,*[9] for example, called it distorting (without giving any specific examples) and said that it labors under the disadvantage of being "frankly feminist," of having an "advocacy stance."[10] She took offense because "the book will certainly arouse anger in women who read it." Good grief (more cartoonery). What sort of Christian faith is afraid of the facts of world history, or unwilling to advocate justice toward women? How mealy-mouthed can the followers of the prophetic Jesus become? I make no apology for standing with the millions of women the religious traditions have abused. Indeed, as Thoreau might have said to Emerson, the question is how other Christians can refuse to stand with them.

THIS BOOK

In the past few pages I have referred to incidents from my own experience, to assure the reader that this book will not be dealing with desiccated, academic matters. Now I want equally to assure the reader that this book is not primarily, or even significantly, a matter of venting my own spleen. It is hard to be a religious feminist today, and anger frequently is the only healthy response. But the real allure that prompts these pages, the real good-held-out, is the prospect of contemplating, and helping to advance, the day when humanistic feminism and deep Christianity see how much they coincide.

At the moment, when so many obstacles and misunderstandings separate her two allegiances, the person of centrist persuasion lives by an omnipresent both/and. Both the insistence of feminism that women be accounted as human as men, and the insistence of Christianity that divine love makes us most human, cry out for acknowledgement. Both indignation that each female dollar is worth only 59¢ in male dollar terms, and indignation that Jesus, Buddha, and Lao Tzu can be scorned as passé (by "men come of age" conflicted with neuroses) cry out for enactment.

However, we must distinguish the present moment from the eschaton. When the kingdom of God has become more manifest, many of our present dualities will merge into unity. Then what Kierkegaard saw as "purity of heart" will come into clearer focus. Purity of heart is to will one thing. It is to attain an honest loving, a loving honesty, that judges all matters by a single standard. Such an honest loving, one suspects, moves the personality to a level above even righteous anger. It "sublates" righteous anger, the Hegelian might say, preserving it but taking it up into a fuller synthesis. The synthesis I foresee will allow feminists and

Christians to deal with one another from the heart. Like Rahner's anonymous Christian agreeing with Nishitani's anonymous Buddhist, it will allow the quality of the players' game, the excellence of the positions' fruits, to predominate over extrinsic names or claims.

Toward this synthesis, I propose a two-way reflection on the major dimensions of reality that any adequate world-view must treat. The major dimensions of reality are nature, society, self, and divinity. None can be considered apart from all the others, without our losing reality's relatedness. None can be collapsed into another, without our losing reality's primal set of distinctions. I am not nature, I am not society, I am not God. Yet, I am not I in isolation from nature, society, or God. Feminism has to deal with this very basic self-presentation of reality, and so does Christianity. The significance of today's woman, and the significance of Jesus today, have equally to be fitted to its four-fold frame. By discussing each dimension from the viewpoint of feminism and Christianity, and by tending toward what Smith calls a "colloquial" point of view ("a side-by-side confronting of the world's problems . . . rather than a face-to-face confronting of each other"),[11] I hope that the purity of heart needed in the future may begin to emerge right now.

Thus the different parts of the book are entitled "Theology," "Psychology," "Sociology," and "Ecology," to indicate which of the four primal dimensions is at the center of the discussion. The discussions themselves should indicate how the four dimensions interrelate, but lest there be any doubt, let me say explicitly that, for the construction of a human world-view, the four are always a reticulation, a multi-connected web.

It is true enough that, in herself, God can exist independently of the world or of human beings. It is true enough that a tree falling in the depths of the forest where there are no human auditors is real and makes a noise. To have significance *for us*, however, God or a natural being must impinge on our consciousness. A being we are unaware of is the same to us as no being at all. And, having impinged on our consciousness, God, nature, society, or the self appears as manifoldly related: to our human consciousness, which can conceive a "God"; to the social shapings of "reality"; to the time and tide none of us can outrun.

Last, since I lashed out at the unfortunate reviewer who criticized my feminism without defining her terms, I should make a final effort to clarify the import that *feminism* and *Christianity* will carry here. By *feminism* I mean the advocacy of women's equality with men, sensitivity to the injustices women have suffered, and the resolution that women come into their own without delay. For example, my feminism notes that women are woefully under-represented in national government, interprets that as a sign of second-class citizenship, and resolves to oppose all who connive in maintaining this unjust status quo. By *Christianity* I mean dependence on Jesus for one's midmost notions of humanity and divinity. They are Christians in substance who take on Christ's lineaments, who repeat (as far as their circumstances allow) Christ's praxis.[12] We shall have plenty of occasion to discuss these lineaments, to try to absorb this praxis. Suffice it to say, for these initial definitions, that Jesus the Christ fused humanity and divinity in terms of love—a passionate love of a parental God with whole mind, heart, soul, and strength, and a passionate love of one's neighbor as oneself.

1/Theology

CHAPTER ONE: THE NEW FOCUS ON THE GODDESS

Let us begin the colloquy between feminism and Christianity with the *thealogy*, the study of feminine divinity, that both feminist scholars in religion and practitioners of a new witchcraft have recently been promoting. The thealogy of feminist scholars in religion has tended to focus on tribal and Eastern divinities, although a wide interpretation could include recent investigations of the feminine attributes of the biblical God.[1] Our first example is Gael Hodgkins's study of Sedna, an Eskimo Goddess.[2] Sedna is physically impressive:

> She is very tall, and has but one eye, which is the left, the place of the other being covered by a profusion of black hair . . . She has one pigtail only, contrary to the established fashion in the upper Eskimaux world . . . and this is of such immense magnitude, that a man can scarcely grasp it with both hands. Its length is exactly twice that of her arm, and it descends to her knees. The hood of her jacket is always worn up (p. 305).

Sedna commands both the animals and human destinies. She lives at the bottom of the ocean, her house guarded by a large, fierce dog. Hodgkins emphasizes the images of depth and creativity with which the myths surround Sedna. She participates in the fathomlessness of the sea and appears as a cosmic genetrix. In these and other ways Sedna represents the Eskimo intuition of transcendence—reality beyond the human and every-day, the mystery of Beginning and Beyond.[3]

If Sedna represents an archaic version of divinity, tied to a shamanistic culture, the female deities of Hinduism represent an almost equally ancient conception—a thealogy spanning the centuries from recent times to prehistory. Rita Gross recently has dealt with these Hindu female deities in terms of several basic images.[4] First, there is the image of the divine couple. Both the Shaivite and Vaishnavite traditions pair their gods, so that male divinity usually has a female consort. The implication obviously is that divinity correlates masculinity and femininity just as humanity does. A more dramatic version of this Hindu conviction occurs in the iconography that presents the gods as hermaphroditic. A statue of Shiva furnishes a good example: "Generally called the Siva Ardhanari icon or 'Siva as half-woman' icon, it is an icon of a single being who is quite obviously male on one side of his body and quite obviously female on the other side of her body, down to the minutest details" (pp. 279-80). Similar instances of hermaphroditic icons occur in the case of Vishnu.

A second basic image that Gross stresses is the coincidence of opposites. Both male and female deities blend creation and destruction, good and bad, birth and death. Kali, for instance, usually appears as black, with fierce eyes and a blood-licking tongue, carrying a severed head and a curved sword. However, other pictures show her in the relaxed pose of a teacher, with gestures of giving peace and granting boons. A third image is the Goddess as Mother. The pictoral emphases on the Goddesses' genitals and breasts underscore the creativity of womanhood. Thus Lakshmi distributes wealth and good fortune, while Sarasvati promotes learning and graceful living. The message here seems to be the wide import of female nurturing.

A more abstract version of feminine divinity occurs in the Buddhist notion that the Perfection of Wisdom (Prajnaparamita) is the "Mother of All Buddhas." Joanna Rogers Macy's study emphasizes that the development of this notion in Mahayana Buddhism permitted "a transcendence of the metaphysical sexual typing that allies the feminine with the arbitrary and devouring forces of nature."[5] Indeed, as the wisdom of a vision from beyond *samsara* (the world of suffering), the Prajnaparamita appears quite disembodied, as "light, emptiness, space, and a *samsara*-confronting gaze that is both clinical and compassionate" (p. 320). As empty (the ultimate mark that Buddhism accords effable reality), She has no self, no substance, no defining characteristics. All these things fall away when one reaches Buddhanature or Nirvana. Still, a certain maternal kindness attaches to the Prajnaparamita. In the form of Tara, the Goddess whom Tibet greatly revered, her many eyes "set in her forehead, hands, and sometimes feet, express her caring and the succor she offers" (p. 321). However, in Mahayana's advanced schools, the Mother of All Buddhas does not call the disciple out of the world. By the dictum that nirvana and samsara are one, she broods a wisdom that sees straightforwardly the "suchness" of things, their actuality. In addition, the Prajnaparamita nurtures the Bodhisattva (saintly) vow of compassion for all beings, so that the disciple gladly lingers in the world to labor for the enlightenment of others.

Thus feminist scholars have been stalking the traces of the Goddess in a variety of cultures. We could point to other foci, such as the East Asian Goddess Kuan-yin,[6] but this should suffice to indicate both current interest and the Goddess's widespread historical influence.

WHY WOMEN NEED THE GODDESS

To understand the new scholarly study of the Goddess and the new witchcraft, one must appreciate the need for self-affirmation that many women feel nowadays. Carol Christ's concluding chapter in *Womanspirit Rising,* "Why Women Need the Goddess," opens with a quotation from a powerful feminist play. As a sort of climactic epiphany the chorus sings, "I found God in myself and I loved her fiercely."[7] In explicating this quotation, Christ first emphasizes the psychic power of symbols, especially those from religious traditions. She then makes the tie to feminism: "Because religion has such a compelling hold on the deep psyches of so many people, feminists cannot afford to leave it in the hands of the fathers. Even people who no longer 'believe in God' or participate in the institutional structure of patriarchal religion still may not be free of the power of the symbolism of God the Father" (p. 274).

Insofar as religion continues to fulfill the important function of helping people to cope with "limit situations" (death, evil, suffering) and to solemnize important transitions (birth, sexuality, death), women continue to feel the need for a religion that gives them support precisely *as* women. Christ argues that traditional Judaism and Christianity cannot give this support, because "religious symbol systems focused around exclusively male images of divinity create the impression that female power can never be fully legitimate or wholly beneficent" (p. 275).

The biblical religions deny the full legitimacy and beneficence of female power by their myths of female evil (for example, the myth of Eve) and by their symbolism of God as male. This leads to a woman's trusting to male power for salvation, distrusting her own female power as inferior or dangerous. The familial and political implications of this include the exaltation of the husband and father, and the "normalcy" of male social leadership. They are a large part of what Simone de Beauvoir had in mind when she wrote, "Man enjoys the great advantage of having a god endorse the code he writes; and since man exercises a sovereign authority over women it is especially fortunate that this authority has been vested in him by the Supreme Being. For the Jew, Mohammedans, and Christians, among others, man is

Master by divine right; the fear of God will therefore repress any impulse to revolt in the downtrodden female."[8] The Goddess therefore emerges as a counterforce, a legitimation of female nature and power. In Christ's fourfold description, Goddess symbolism arouses new religious feelings that affirm women's power, their bodies, their wills, and their bonds and heritage.

Out of the prehistoric past, when female deities were worshiped across a wide swath of civilizations, today's feminists are self-consciously selecting powerful role models who can ground female nature in the cosmic scheme of things. By linking women to a female sacral power, the new Goddess-devotee is affirming herself, saying that what makes God God is as much in her as in men. More important than the question of the Goddess's objective reality, then, is her symbolic function, and one can expect that future thealogians will be more sensitive to Goddess symbolism than past theologians have been.

Concerning women's bodies, the Goddess tends to work a long-needed boost in self-esteem. Many cultures have denigrated the female body as more carnal than the male, or have even considered it "polluted" because of its menstrual flow of blood. Women thus have been pressured to feel dirty. The tendency of Goddess religion is to exalt female creativity and cyclicism. The Goddess is the prime symbol of life-bearing, nurturing, waxing and waning. She says that blood, childbearing, nursing, flowing and ebbing are the quintessence of living Being.

A third important implication of the Goddess symbolism is the positive representation of will that Goddess-centered rituals advance. Here the supporting notion is that the Goddess personifies the energies that flow through the natural and human worlds, energies that can be tapped by ritual magic. Such ritual magic involves an affirmation of female will power that contrasts sharply with the submissiveness to which women traditionally have been trained. The Goddess therefore calls women to a strength and independence many have never known before.

Fourth, Christ sees the Goddess as a focus for female bonding, and for a new appreciation of women's traditions. As an ultimate symbol, the Goddess supports female friendship and collaboration, while the ancient past out of which she comes stands forth as a treasury of women's poetry, healing rites, sisterly gatherings, and celebrations of life. Against the prevailing view that only men make culture or do important deeds, the Goddess says that women have long done marvelous deeds, long glimpsed splendid beauty.

THE NEW WITCHCRAFT

The Spiral Dance,[9] by the feminist witch Starhawk, is a fine exposition of the rituals and theory that translate the supposedly ancient traditions about the Goddess into a contemporary religion for women (and men). Starhawk is explicit that the Goddess centers this religion:

> The primary symbol for "That-Which-Cannot-Be-Told" is the Goddess. The Goddess has infinite aspects and thousands of names—She is the reality behind many metaphors. She *is* reality, the manifest deity, omnipresent in all of life, in each of us. The Goddess is not separate from the world—She *is* the world, and all things in it: moon, sun, earth, star, stone, seed, flowing river, wind, wave, leaf and branch, bud and blossom, fang and claw, woman and man. In Witchcraft, flesh and spirit are one (p. 8).

Witchcraft usually gathers adherents into small cells called covens. Thirteen is the maximum number, so that members can balance communal sharing and individual experience. At meetings the group enacts time-honored rituals that create a sacred space by "casting a circle."

> Goddess and God are then invoked or awakened within each participant and considered to be physically present within the circle and the bodies of the worshippers. Power, the subtle force that shapes reality, is raised through chanting or dancing and may be directed through a symbol or visualization. With the raising of

the cone of power comes ecstasy, which may then lead to a trance state in which visions are seen and insights gained (p. 14).

In Starhawk's view, the coven rituals ultimately express a paleolithic, shamanic outlook. For that outlook, things are basically swirls of energy, waves of a single, ever-changing energy sea. The fixity and separateness we ordinarily find in things is but part of a larger story. Much as modern physics presents a more dynamic, interactive view of reality than does common sense, so Witchcraft proposes an extra-ordinary mode of perception that stresses patterns and relationships, rather than individual, separated objects. This holistic perception is "the mode of starlight: dim and silvery, revealing the play of woven branches and the dance of shadows, sensing pathways as spaces in the whole" (p. 18).

Many of the Craft's training exercises aim at awakening this holistic, starlight vision. Focusing on the lability of nature, and giving special attributes to such phenomena as the compass directions, the seasons, and the primal elements (earth, air, fire, and water), the exercises express a world-view similar to that of American Indians or traditional Africans, who also have tried to see nature whole. Stressing imagination, the Craft, like ancient shamanic traditions, tries to draw upon the power of the natural elements with which the human person, body and spirit, is ecological.

Modern Craft members often do this with an explicit psychology in mind. Drawing on the Faery Tradition, they speak of the unconscious mind as Younger Self, the conscious mind as Talking Self, and the immanent divinity as High Self. Each psychological dimension has its truth and good function; the ideal is harmony among the three. But since current Western culture neglects Younger Self, most of the Craft's exercises seem designed to free the unconscious—to promote spontaneity, play, and the loosening of controls, so as to gain a greater feeling of unity with nature, of oneness between body and spirit.

For Starhawk, divinity is best symbolized through a conjunction of the Goddess and the Horned God. The

Goddess's beauty glimmers in the traditional charge she gives her devotees: "Hear the words of the Star Goddess, the dust of whose feet are the hosts of heaven, whose body encircles the universe: 'I am the beauty of the green earth and the white moon among the stars and the mysteries of the waters, I call upon your soul to arise and come unto me. For I am the soul of nature that gives life to the universe'" (pp. 76-77). Above all, the Goddess fosters love and natural pleasure. She calls her adherents to see her in all facets of natural life, and to accept all: the rotation of the seasons, the circle of life and death, the times for rejoicing and the times for lamenting. Each part of the cosmic dance has its beauty, its necessity, its wisdom. The Goddess is the earth that brings forth life, but she is also the air and the waters. The moon is her special symbol, and women are her images, but she lives also in men.

The Horned God complements the symbolisms of the Goddess. He sanctifies masculinity, but not as many Westerners might expect:

> The image of the Horned God in Witchcraft is radically different from any other image of masculinity in our culture. He is difficult to understand, because He does not fit into any of the expected stereotypes, neither those of the "macho" male nor the reverse-images of those who deliberately seek effeminacy. He is gentle, tender, and comforting, but He is also the Hunter. He is the Dying God—but his death is always in the service of the life force. He is untamed sexuality—but sexuality as a deep, holy, connecting power. He is the power of feeling, and the image of what men could be if they were liberated from the constraints of patriarchal culture (p. 94).

AGAINST ABSOLUTISM

When Starhawk projects the future directions in which the Craft should take the Goddess religion, she stresses an inclusive attitude quite different from the absolutism she thinks afflicts the patriarchal religions. Part of this absolutism comes from confusing symbols with reality. The patriarchal religions tend to collapse the descriptions they have fashioned with the divine order itself. The result is a mentality of antitheses. Either the biblical description of God's creation of Adam and Eve is true, or the description by Darwinian science is true. They cannot both stand. This absolutist attitude can continue even when the patriarchal religions themselves have been abandoned. Thus one can find Freudians ranged against Marxists, and feminists who emphasize spirituality ranged against feminists who emphasize politics.

The Goddess religion offers a way out of these antitheses, because it stresses the immanence of divinity, its spread through all creation. The result tends to be an attitude of synthesis. An intelligent witch easily sees, for example, that both *a priori* categories of consciousness and *a posteriori* material conditions affect our struggle to be whole. Indeed, as many of the Eastern religions have seen, wholeness itself is a matter of harmony among different polarities, of graceful movement to a variegated flow.

By contrast, the tendency of the Western traditions to adopt an antithetical mentality has fashioned many a rigid dualism. One form of this dualism has been what Starhawk calls the "Chosen People Syndrome." The Chosen People think their way is the sole truth. The ways of other people are wrong. Indeed, the ways of other people are taking them to damnation, so both the other people and their foreign ways must be evil. At the extreme, "We are excused from recognizing their humanness and from treating them according to the ethics with which we treat each other. Generally, the Chosen People set about the task of purifying themselves from any contact with the carriers of evil. When they are in power, they institute inquisitions, Witchhunts, pogroms, executions, censorship, and concentration camps" (p. 189).

Even the women's movement has inherited some of this thinking, for many feminists argue in a separatist vein. Like other oppressed and powerless groups who have thought they possessed the truth, some feminist circles have thought they could only be "pure" by removing themselves from the larger community. To this tendency Starhawk answers with a distinction. She would allow a certain separation, calculated to give women a space of their own in which to recover from the hurts inflicted by men and to probe their own special concerns. But a radical withdrawal from the larger society, a separatism strictly so called, runs counter to the universal presence of the Goddess. The Goddess is bound up with the lives of men as well as women. She reveals herself in the experiences of heterosexual women as well as homosexual, of active mothers as well as solitary virgins.

Behind this balanced judgment is the conviction that a matrifocal culture rooted in the Goddess celebrates diversity. Diversity is nature's habit, nature's method of assuring survival and continuing evolution. The great proliferation of different species, and the almost unimaginable reticulation of the ecological web, are all arguments that diversity is at the core of natural reality. Overspecialization tends to produce narrowness and inflexibility, which are the highways to extinction. The lesson for political and spiritual movements should be obvious. They must encourage diversity if they are to survive and prosper. Staying clear of the Chosen People Syndrome, they should aim at creating a "religion of heretics," of people who refuse to toe ideological lines or support doctrines of exclusivity.

Starhawk's future Witchcraft also would espouse science. Recognizing the differences between science and magic, it would be open to science's more rigorous ways of exploring the mysteries of the universe. Without denying the paramount need of our rationalistic culture to retrieve holistic modes of perception, her future Witchcraft would learn all it could from current scientific probings, for the stuff with which they all deal is, finally, the Goddess. Moreover, by staying in contact with science, Witchcraft might better influence the emotional side of our relationships with nature. For example, if it were legitimate to regard the oceans not simply as reservoirs of chemicals but also as "our Mother, the womb of life," we might be less inclined to pollute the oceans.

These and Starhawk's other strivings for nuance show that the new Witchcraft is far from simpleminded. In its better representatives, it is well aware of the dangers of superstition, quite on guard against psychological imbalance and pathology. Trying to rehabilitate femininity, sexuality, emotion, imagination, and the other parts of human nature that modern culture has repressed, the new Witchcraft would reforge our bonds with nature, reknit the different social classes. In its final sketches of what Craft members might be doing in the future, Starhawk's *Spiral Dance* is reminiscent of Ernest Callenbach's *Ecotopia.*[10] Her witches would be celebrating the lifecycle and nature, the body and the egalitarian group.

CHRISTIAN REFLECTIONS I

One needs only a minimal openness to the God who has left traces everywhere, and a minimal awareness of Western culture's current spiritual needs, to feel great sympathy for the feminist revival of the Goddess religion. For the modern human person, this religion's stresses on play, love, imagination, ecology, and healthy sex are timely indeed. For women, its stresses on the feminine side of divinity, sisterhood, the beauty of the female body, the rightness of female will-power, and the like are profoundly therapeutic. A sacramental Christianity, sensitive to the ways divinity fills the natural world, can affirm most of the new Goddess religion. A Christianity self-critical and pluralistic would offer the new witches space in which to grow their fruits, so that what their religion finally carries might be seen fairly.

Nonetheless, there are considerable differences between the Goddess religion and Christianity, so probing the points of divergence in the two systems is essential for an honest colloquy. The two major points of divergence I find regard transcendence and salvation: whether divinity is more than the natural world, and how we are to conceive of, and combat, evil. Before dealing with these two major points, however, let me mention another point, the relation between myth and history. Like most points in a "system," it can be taken to the heart of the world-view, but I can treat it only in passing.

The Goddess religion tends to prize myth more than history. What the Goddess was in the past is often unrecoverable, but even when it is, most witches value such history less than what the Goddess means today psychologically, as a cluster of stories and symbols. We shall deal with psychology more in the next part, but it seems important to note here that a great deal of current feminist religion deliberately functions as a psychology, a shaping of women's self-consciousness.[11] History and ontology ("reality" in a trans-personal sense) are less important than myth.

This tendency has much to teach Christianity, but perhaps it also leaves feminists with something to learn. For example, the feminist prizing of myth and psychology seems to blur the comparisons that the Goddess religion ought to be making between itself and the patriarchal religions. Where the comparison ought to be myth to myth and history to history, it often compares history to myth. Thus, the historical treatment of witches by Christians (a valid enough topic) is compared to the Craft's symbols of equality and pluralism, rather than being compared to how the Craft itself actually has treated people, especially deviants, in the far or recent past. Feminist analyses of the Christian symbol-system often are rather naïve, and the Craft tends to ignore Christianity's historical claims, assuming rather than proving that the Jesus story is essentially mythical. As an enormously sophisticated literature now shows,[12] the Jesus story is both myth and history. Certainly, however, it is historical enough to deserve a critico-sympathetic treatment, especially regarding Jesus' death and resurrection.

Obviously, this question of myth and history relates to the points I want to examine more fully: salvation and transcendence. To begin with salvation, the question goes to the heart of the Christian delineation of the problem of evil and its solution. For the Christian delineation of the problem of evil and its solution stems from the axial part of Jesus' story, his death and resurrection. Convinced that there is a solid historical nucleus to the reports of Jesus' death and resurrection, most Christian theology has probed the problem of evil more realistically, and I would say more profoundly, than the Goddess religion does.

The tendency of Goddess religion is to accept the negative along with the positive, seeing both as part of nature's scheme. This neither promotes an unblinking look at human malice, nor squares well with the judgments the Craft makes about the evils it is to avoid or try to extirpate. Why are human malice, misogynism, and pathology not just part of the natural scheme? Who is to say the Goddess did not want the persecutions of witches, that they were not just a social analogue to the forest fires, earthquakes, cancers, and other destructive occurrences that have long purged natural history? If the ultimate reality embraces death as well as life, evil as well as good, there is some illogic in a religious opposition to death and evil. Christianity can join the Goddess religion in sponsoring life. (Irenaeus' "The glory of God is human beings fully alive; the life of human beings is the vision of God" comes to mind.)[13] Can the Goddess religion join Christianity in fighting evil and claiming a conquest of death?

To be sure, many other questions shout for consideration. The love *(agape)* that Christians say took Jesus to his cross and ultimately conquered death has not been sufficiently evident in Christian history to make the Christian solution to the problem of evil easily credible. Even apart from this historical failure, Christianity involves a *faith* that distinguishes it somewhat from the supposedly empirical stance of good witches. The precise nature of this distinction is a nice question, but it need not concern us here. Here I only want to suggest that, despite all its dangers, there is something positive, indeed necessary, in the Christian view of evil.

CHRISTIAN REFLECTIONS II

Thinking that Jesus is God's decisive say about the human condition (as well as humanity's best cipher for the divine condition), Christians have spoken of a singular good news and grace. We shall note some of the contemporary accents to this speech in the next chapter, but the point here is their bearing on the question of salvation. The "salvation" that Goddess religion offers is the fruit of self-awakening and attunement. Calling forth more of herself, the devotee escapes many causes of disease, depression, and failure. Growing more attuned to the cosmic powers, she lives with less conflict and more peace. This is an estimable salvation, but it does not go to the depths of the Christian claim. For the Christian claim is that Jesus is the absolute savior, the eschatological revelation of divine love and power.[14] In Jesus' life, death, and resurrection God has supposedly broken the human bondage to evil, shown once and for all the abounding of grace over sin. Bracketing for the moment the question of whether Christians' lives have made this claim credible, let us probe the claim itself.

The claim relates to the Christian conception that evil has no part in God. Neither malice nor death cohere with divinity. Building on the prophetic portions of scripture, current liberation theologians picture God as laboring for the defeat of human malice, while past dogmatic theologians pictured God as laboring to take human beings up into divine deathlessness. Schillebeeckx roots the current picture in the original Christian experience:

> The Christian experience which an originally Jewish group of people had of Jesus of Nazareth developed into the confession that for these men, whom originally only outsiders called "Christians," the painful and humanly insoluble question of the purpose and the meaning of life as man in nature and history, in a context of meaning and meaninglessness, of elements of sorrow and joy, had been given a positive and unique "answer," exceeding all expectations: God himself had guaranteed that

> human life would have a positive and meaningful significance. He himself had staked his honour on it, and that honour was his identification with the outcast, with the exploited, with the enslaved, above all the sinner, i.e. the man who so hurts his fellow man and himself that this hurt "cries out to heaven."[15]

Despite its embarrassingly sexist language, the quotation expresses a singular point. The Christian God is not equipoised between evil and good, negativity and positivity. The Christian God is light in whom there is no darkness at all, goodness in whom there is no evil at all. As the emissary and revelation of this God, Jesus fought against the bedrock evil of human lovelessness. On this point Christians and witches can largely agree: love is the "cure" for most human ills. But, in my opinion, the suffering love of the biblical God goes deeper, to the heart of the problematic. By what Bernard Lonergan has called "the law of the cross,"[16] Jesus' suffering-love stops the cycle of tit for tat, hate for hate. Empowered by God, it answers evil with good.

Empirically, individual witches may do a better job at living this thesis than individual Christians. All that we said in the Introduction about the criterion of "fruits," and about anonymous Christianity, remains in force. Theoretically, in terms of basic notions and symbols, Christianity attacks the problem of evil better than the feminist religion I have seen. And this relates to the problem of transcendence, for the problem of evil/salvation leads on to the question of a trans-cosmic deity. One can see this (perhaps more dispassionately) in the cases of Hinduism and Buddhism. The problem of suffering there leads to *moksha* and *nirvana:* states that transcend the world of *karma* and *samsara.* Even when one gets to the sophisticated dialectics of Madhyamika, the Buddhist school that helped Confucian East Asia retain a this-wordly stress (by showing how *nirvana* and *samsara* are one), a nisus for transcendence remains. At the least, the Prajnaparamita plays at the outermost edges of cosmic reality, at the verge of creation from nothingness.[17]

By the conjunction of biblical revelation and Greek

philosophy, Western religion separated true divinity from the cosmos. As a result, it carried a four-fold image of reality, the schema of nature, society, self, and divinity that I outlined in the Introduction.[18] Thus, Christianity (and Judaism and Islam) have refused to identify divinity with either the physical world, or the human psyche, or the social group. Only a trans-cosmic, trans-psychic, trans-social God could work the salvation they have found revelation to imply. Once again, of course, I must note that each of these points would have to be developed very carefully, so that a proper modesty about the theoretical clarity Christianity claims, and an even greater modesty about the Christian performance historically, would come into play. The kindly question for feminist religion, though, is whether the Goddess does not represent something of an intellectual regression, for all that she may represent an emotional advance.[19] Even after viewing Goddess worship kindly as "iconolatry,"[20] I find that the "beyond" of the Western God cries out to be taken into account.

CHAPTER TWO: THE NEW FOCUS ON JESUS

Assuming that our colloquy is well under way, starting to push out the tendrils that make organic connections, let us turn to a Christian equivalent of the recent feminist focus on the Goddess. Recently the "beyond" of the Christian God has riveted onto the person of Jesus of Nazareth in a way that advances the traditional pattern of Christian theology another turn of the helix. The traditional pattern of Christian theology, I assume, has centered in the Incarnation. When asked for their core theo-logy, their core sense of what ultimate reality is like and how it comports itself, Christians have pointed to Jesus Christ. From New Testament times, Jesus has been their *Ursakrament*—their primal symbol for divinity. By the time of the great church councils (fourth to sixth centuries), this primal symbolism had come to mean Jesus' "hypostatic" union of a full humanity with the full divinity of the Logos. Pressured by modern epistemology, and by such post-modern trends as an increased awareness of the other world religions, present-day Christian theologians have been probing anew the flesh, person, and speech of this man whose identity their tradition has thought so indicative of God.

There are tons of literature from the various schools of the new quest for the historico-parabolic Jesus. I can only draw on a few studies that offer contact points with religious feminism. Samuel Terrien's *The Elusive Presence,*[1] for instance, lays a boardwalk to all sorts of people initially "non-Christian" yet open to divine mystery, by interpreting the overall biblical notion of God mystagogically—as a fullness that human faculties never can master. Terrien's lead sentence gives the thesis to which his long career of biblical scholarship has led:

> The reality of the presence of God stands at the center of biblical faith. This presence, however, is always elusive. "Verily, verily, thou art a God that hidest thyself!" The Deity of the Hebrew-Christian Scriptures escapes man's grasp and manipulation, but man is aware of the presence of that Deity in such a powerful way that he finds through it a purpose in the universe; he confers upon his own existence a historical meaning; and he attunes his selfhood to an ultimate destiny (p. xxvii).

Terrien displays this thesis through a full investigation of the major literary units of the Hebrew Bible, and then he continues on to the New Testament materials. As a link between the two testaments, he lays it down that "the church began as a Jewish sect which hailed Jesus as the Lord, for it saw in him the human mirror of God himself" (p. 410). Reinterpreting the notion of divine presence in terms of Jesus, the evangelists focused on the annunciation, transfiguration, and resurrection to stress that Jesus was a new theophany, temple, and epiphany. The Johannine Prologue furnished all subsequent Christianity an anchor to Jesus' flesh by fixing God's "glory" to it. "When the hymnist sang 'And we have seen his glory,' he testified that 'the Word' had lived on this earth at a particular time, and he confided that he had sensorially perceived the most extraordinary spectacle: Divine Wisdom inseparable in his mind from the Divine Word was seen in the flesh of a man. The presence of God was for a time contained in a human person" (p. 420).

This high point of divine manifestation, however, never removed the divine mystery. It could not, for God is never really God if finite senses and intelligences can comprehend her. But the anamnesis of past manifestations, past fleeting glimpses of the divine presence or hearings of the divine speech, became a hermeneutics for present existence.

"When God no longer overwhelmed the senses of perception and concealed himself behind the adversity of historical existence, those who accepted the promise were still aware of God's nearness in the very veil of his seeming absence. For them, the center of life was a *Deus absconditus atque praesens*" (p. 470). The Christian turn of this Hebraic conviction simply focused it on Jesus: "Christianity became distinct from Judaism when a handful of men and women saw the sign of the final epiphany not only in the teaching and the healing deeds of Jesus but also in the totality of his person, dying and alive" (p. 471). For Christians, the God hidden and present had but further clarified the divine promise, but further specified her signatory "I am as I shall be with you" (Exod. 3:14) in Jesus the Christ.

A dozen implications leap to mind. Perhaps most relevant for our colloquy are: 1) the biblical affirmation of God's ineluctable mystery, which assures that no person ever will have divine truth in her pocket. At a stroke, divine mystery devastates both fundamentalism and dogmatism, enforcing on all biblical religionists a profound humility.[2] 2) The sacramental character of human being. For Christians, the prime revelation of the divine presence is in the flesh of a human being. This must not lead to a denigration of physical nature, and it must not interpret "human being" to the prejudice of women. When the Genesis account of creation echoes through it properly, however, a dazzling theandricity steps forth. Humanness is God's best cipher. 3) We should exploit the variety of the biblical impressions of divine mystery in this mystagogic mood, especially those that carry feminine overtones, such as Lady Wisdom and the brooding Spirit. 4) The correlative of biblical mystagogy is biblical contemplation. One will find little of God's elusive (sacramental) presence if one is stupid in the ways of prayer.

MORAL TRANSCENDENCE

One also will find little of God's elusive presence if one is self-seeking in things broadly political. The God who impels

Jesus to proclaim the Beatitudes is no sanctioner of the pseudo-Christian utilitarianism driving the current-day West. Edward Schillebeeckx has sketched the lineage of this utilitarianism:

> Modern analyses have made it clear that our Western society has in fact been governed—and is still governed—by the ideals of "utilitarian individualism." This view was formulated for the first time, rather crudely, in the Enlightenment by Thomas Hobbes, and afterwards rather more subtly by John Locke (who camouflaged the tension between it and the Christian gospel); it was translated into economic terms by Adam Smith. In the version propounded by Locke, this view is the soul of all modern Western society: a neutral state in which the individual can strive to maximize his own interest; the end product of this is expected to be the private and public welfare of each and everyone.[3]

The tension between Locke and Jesus grows taut indeed in Paul Ricoeur's Christology. For Ricoeur, Jesus manifests a God whose "morals" are as far above our selfishness as the heavens are above the earth.[4] Indeed, there is a largesse to God's gift of Jesus, a prodigality, that staggers all but the most leaden observer. Jesus' own parabolic speech seems designed to evoke this moral transcendence of his God. The story of the prodigal son (Luke 15) is perhaps the most famous example, but Jesus' whole preaching rings with the same message: my Abba is not the safe, calculable Father-figure you, my hearers, may imagine. My Abba stands more with the last than with the first. He blesses the have-nots more than the comfortable. Children, women, and sinners are more apt to open to my Abba's knocking than are the "great men" of any establishment. The poor "people of the land," the publicans, and the whores are more apt to welcome his messenger than are the priests and vintners.

This largesse, contradiction of secular society's expectations, and hyperbole come to a flash point in Jesus' death. It is scandalous, a thrust to the jugular of the almost invincible human tendency to domesticate God. The God whom Jesus manifests suffers and dies because of his identification with humanity's outcastes. Building on its high reading of Jesus' union with the Logos, the tradition allowed such fillips as "God died on the cross."[5] It went on to ponder Jesus' death as both God's loving demonstration of the depths of human evil, and God's loving conquest of human evil. In extending Jesus' mission to the embrace of death, God worked death's defeat. The resurrection symbolized Jesus' passover to the deathlessness of God. Ratifying the way Jesus had walked, and the message Jesus had preached, God's taking of Jesus to herself compounded the scandal of the cross. If the crucifixion was a stumbling block to the Jews, the resurrection was to the Gentiles but foolishness.

Ricoeur's Christology therefore runs in the lineaments of the Pauline *kenosis* (Phil. 2:5-11). The God it hymns goes further in love than we human beings find comfortable. He has a moral "beyond" that is parallel to his ontological "beyond." In his doing and judging he stands outside secular canons, recreating order, possibility, and hope from the nothingness of human malice. I find this socially disruptive Christology immensely liberating. It explodes the arrogant superiority of the world's movers and shakers. Mercy, conversion, and justice are what Jesus' God wants (on the latter, Christians and Marxists can roundly agree[6]). She cares nothing for money or social status. If pushed to a single word, her desideratum is only love. To build one's life, one's society, one's culture on other foundations is to build on sand.

Now, it seems to me that this reading of Christian "morality" both supports current feminism and chastens it. It supports women as equal to men, for its God is no respecter of outer persons. It sunders the ideological self-preservation behind most institutional sexism, for it pushes forward, not a Christ of power, but a Christ emptied of power, a Christ anointed for suffering service. It has a message of profound hope for all the planet's dispossessed, for it presents God as a liberator from sin and mortality, from injustice and death-dealing. Insofar as women cry out for justice, they join Jesus' prayer of abandonment. Insofar as they open to possibilities beyond what secular imagination suggests, they wait on recreative grace. Insofar as they put their shoulders to the wheel, opposing the selfishness and avarice of the male-dominated American 1984, they do the essentially prophetic deed, in the footsteps of the one Christians call the eschatological prophet.

On the other hand, insofar as current feminists may be seduced by visions of the Lockean good life, be aiming no higher than access to establishmentarian power, the morality of Jesus' God nay-says them. Those are not the ways to peace and true prosperity. Later we shall come to the feminist discussion of women's sins, at which point I shall explain my agreement with the current tendency to look for failings other than pride. But the humanistic depth I see in the Christology of Ricoeur and his like forbids my agreeing with feminist self-development uncritically. Jesus' God nurtures, sponsors, and celebrates a healthy self-love. She herself is such an ardent lover, however, that she would raze all shabby huts of egocentricity, whatever their gender or material. As the mystics have found, God is a living flame of love that purifies in order to complete. Her blazing against evil and comforting in the dark are of a piece.

CHRISTIAN FREEDOM

The concern of the Christian God for human beings' welfare is susceptible of quite contemporary interpretations. Thus a well-informed Christology such as William Thompson's *Jesus, Lord and Savior,*[7] influenced by current process thought, by the work of the Jewish theologian Abraham Heschel on the prophets, and by feminism, stresses God's *pathos* (receptive-suffering love). In Thompson's reading,

Jesus reveals a God intimately related to the world, a God whose love for her creation leads to a freely chosen divine vulnerability. Langdon Gilkey's *Message and Existence*[8] also emphasizes God's involvement and self-chosen limitation. So the attunement of today's theologians to Jesus' own speech about God, along with their search for a more dynamic ontology, has led most to distance themselves from classical models in which divine sovereignty threatened to crush human freedom. Today, intimacy with God is seen as encouraging human autonomy, for God is seen as the prime laborer on human freedom's behalf.

Edward Schillebeeckx's massive project in Christology is a landmark in the effort to tie such a systematic theology to scriptural exegesis. In the middle of his *Christ: The Experience of Jesus as Lord*[9] occurs a summary section on how grace and salvation early expressed themselves as liberation. Since feminism is perhaps the most powerful of the current liberation movements, the section carries a special relevance for our colloquy. Schillebeeckx opens it by observing that New Testament Christianity was not content to deal in generalities: "The New Testament adds specific detail to the Christian experience of redemption, salvation and liberation, by defining what Christians feel themselves to be freed from and for what they know themselves to be free" (p. 512).

The "from," or *terminus a quo,* of Christian freedom includes sin and guilt, existential anxieties (above all, the fear of demons), the grip of fate, anxieties about death, everyday concerns, sorrow, despair, hopelessness, dissatisfactions with fellow human beings, dissatisfactions with God, lack of freedom, unrighteousness, oppressive and alienating ties, lovelessness, arbitrariness, egotism, credulity, mercilessness toward others, concern for reputation, cutting a good figure, panic, absence of pleasure, and more. It is a long list, implying a very complete liberation. All that mildewed human life, that caused suffering and fear, had in principle been cast aside. By God's grace, a "new being" stood forth unshackled, no longer a slave. Jesus had preached "The Kingdom of God," apparently meaning a new era, when all things would be well. The early disciples of Jesus felt they had entered the Kingdom, had left the *ancien régime* where so many things were ill. At core, one senses a loss of paralyzing dread. The dark side of the psyche had yielded to the sun of justice.

The "for what" or *terminus ad quem* of Christian freedom included righteousness, peace with one's fellow human beings, peace with God, a new creation, the restoration of all things, joy, happiness, life, eternal glory, love, hope, sanctification, purification from sin, zeal for all good things, commitment to what was noble, generosity, warmth, equality, sharing of goods, imitation of God, walking in love as Christ walked, and more. In sum, salvation gave healing, being made whole and right. Through their faith, the creators of the New Testament had found the substance of human fulfillment. They proclaimed a joyous "good news" because the agonies of the past were over, the future stretched fair and free.

Still, Schillebeeckx makes sure that some realism about the remaining imperfections of human existence seeps through this euphoria:

> Liberation from various forms of human slavery and the fear of death is both the *consequence* of the adoption of grace or birth from God and also the *requirement* of this grace. In other words, liberation is not only liberation from unjust conditions *for* something good; what men are freed *for* is itself in turn a command to free men from unjust circumstances. For it is redemption within a world which is still damaged and sick. All this indicates that redemption and liberation in the New Testament are both a gift and a task to be realized (p. 513).

The key phrase that should echo as Christians try to realize such liberation is the Johannine *nenikeka:* "I have overcome the world" (John 16:33). When the gap between the New

Testament description of freedom and human beings' continuing enslavements yawns especially wide, this phrase may turn quite bitter-sweet. But the gap is not so inductive of cynicism as a facile political science might assume. Were the core symbolism of Jesus' death-resurrection to be taken to heart, were Jesus' central commandment of love to be obeyed passionately, the human condition could change very rapidly. As the saints of all traditions clearly show, the power for such transformation is ever at hand. The main surd of our situation is why human beings find it so hard to believe, hope, and love—why saintliness is something exceptional.

JESUS' SECRET

Jesus' own obedience to the commandment of love is probably the best key to the recesses of his personality. In a beautiful, simple study,[10] the Dutch scripture scholar Lucas Grollenberg has employed this key most effectively. He begins his probe of Jesus' "mystery" by noting that Jews contemporary with Jesus had a recent tradition of being interested in their God's universal import. As a result, they tended to understand their covenant and election as a call to play a part in a larger scheme. In fact, they thought of themselves as the servants of the nations' chance to recognize the one God as creator and king. Building on this foundation, Jesus developed his own universalist sense of divinity. "Jesus believed that the God of Israel wrote no one off or, in positive terms, that the mystery denoted by the word 'God' is a love which goes out to everyone and seeks to embrace all men. He felt himself called, 'elected' to express this love and make it a decisive factor in human relationships" (p. 103).

In many ways, Jesus' expression of his vocation placed him in the tradition of the Hebrew prophets. He was much like Hosea, for instance, in believing that God so loved His people He would never write them off. But was this assurance not more than what a familiarity with the prophets, or even an ardent embrace of the prophets, could have produced? For Grollenberg, it was indeed:

> Jesus' utter assurance seems to come from this sense of being loved by God. He even addressed God as Abba, which is quite extraordinary. Jewish children used the word as an affectionate way of addressing their fathers, rather as English children say "daddy." It would not have entered the head of any grown-up Jew to use the word when praying to the holy God of Israel. When a Jew said "father," "my (or our) Father," in his prayers, he always added a phrase like ". . . and my (or our) king," to avoid being too familiar and to keep his distance (p. 106).

It is possible to understand Jesus' theme of the Kingdom in terms of this intimate, filial love. In speaking of the coming Kingdom, Jesus was describing a time when *all* people might feel toward God the perfect trust that he himself felt. Then, human relationships might transpire in wholehearted trust, as a sort of redundancy from people's regarding God as their Abba. So the *metanoia* Jesus called for, the conversion, was a turning away from distrust, a turning toward a divinity utterly parental. The newness of the Kingdom was God's writing "quits" under the people's past history, so that a fair future might weigh more than the troubled past. Whereas in past times, narrow laws such as the *lex talionis,* the law of "eye for eye and tooth for tooth," had constricted social life, in future times, the active impress of God's loving ways might renovate social life. If God treated human beings lovingly, human beings ought to treat one another lovingly. Floating on a reservoir of trust in God, the converted personality might move toward her fellow human beings trustingly. At the extreme, Jesus' followers were to draw from their trust in God the strength to forgive other people "seventy times seven." As their Abba took the slightest evidence of repentance as a warrant for forgiving them, so they were to take the slightest evidence of their neighbor's repentance as a warrant for forgiving her.

Naturally enough, Jesus' hearers found this idealistic message hard to accept. It implied an end to self-assertion, a detachment from material possessions, and a bracketing of concern for status and achievement, because such things tend to interfere with egalitarian love and forgiveness. To remove such things left a person hanging over a void, unless she had faith in (and behind faith, surely, intense experience of) a God as good as Jesus'. Only utter confidence in his Abba allowed Jesus to preach and live as he did. "When Jesus' disciples told him that he was asking for the moon, that people would never give up what they had, he simply replied, 'For God nothing is impossible'" (p. 106).

From one point of view, of course, Jesus' disciples have been proved right. In the ongoing showdown between the Dostoyevskian Grand Inquisitor and Christ, the majority of people apparently choose the "security" of the Grand Inquisitor's direction of their lives, at least so far as outward things are concerned. "We have corrected Thy work and have founded it upon *miracle, mystery,* and *authority*. And men rejoiced that they were again led like sheep, and that the terrible gift that brought them such suffering, was, at last, lifted from their hearts" (Dostoyevski, *The Brothers Karamazov*). However, the failure of this sort of prudent politics to make just societies, let alone to express the Kingdom, is a powerful argument *e contrario*. The negative results of the neglect of Jesus' call for trusting love show forth its truth dramatically.

Jesus was willing to die for his faith in his Abba, and to live boldly in the amazing freedom it gave. His faith made him a personality so strong he could both wither the prevailing social authorities and deal with pariahs gently, healingly. Secure in God's love, Jesus "put the primal forces which ordinary mortals use in self-defence at the service of other people" (p. 112). He could give and give, because his ultimate resource was unfathomable. At the end, Christians found that Jesus' love proved stronger than death. For them, the resurrection was the Abba's final, most dazzling display of the divine trustworthiness. Giving himself over to God utterly, Jesus was taken into the divine *athanasia,* the divine deathlessness.

FEMINIST REFLECTIONS I

In the preface to her study of women's experience and the theologies of Reinhold Niebuhr and Paul Tillich,[11] Judith Plaskow has issued something of a lament:

> I find it disappointing that other women more involved than I in the struggle with traditional religion have not taken up Valerie Saiving's cudgel and attempted to write systematic theology from a feminist perspective. It seems that so much reformist energy has been channeled into more immediate tasks—the fight for ordination, liturgical reform, reinterpretation of Scripture—that there has not been time for consideration of this fundamental and difficult issue (p. vii).

Valerie Saiving's cudgel lashed out particularly at the biases in male theologians' notions of sin. Where it might be accurate to label the central male failing as pride, or "will to power," Saiving saw women tending to sin by triviality and diffuseness—by underdevelopment of the self, rather than overdevelopment.[12] Finding this intriguing, I propose some loosely systematic reflections on the relation of Saiving's view to the love of Jesus we have just seen.

In Grollenberg's interpretation of Jesus, love of God (with whole mind, heart, soul, and strength) translated into a complete trust. The result, however, was no underdevelopment of the self, no passivity that was debilitating. Indeed, the second part of Jesus' agapeic program was an intense love of neighbor (as oneself). For this second part, trust in God was a foundation, and self-love was a model. Reassessing Jesus' preaching with a feminist eye, today's theologian would do well to stress the balance, the median character, of the self-love that Christian faith ought to develop. The theological underpinning for the healthy psychology we shall be pursuing in Part II is a view of virtue as a golden mean, and a view of sin as a missing of this mean.

"Virtue," of course, etymologically implies power. When one has good moral health, when one is holy, one's character is strong and effective. For Christians, Jesus himself will always be the prime exemplar of theological virtue, and any portrait of Jesus that is faithful to the New Testament will show him to be a powerful character. By contrast, sin connotes the absence of good moral health. In sin the personality is diseased, disordered, characteristically weak and ineffective in the things that make for peace, justice, and the other ingredients of human prospering. The sinner may have immense physical or psychic energy, but her missing the mean of right relation to God and neighbor makes her a cause of woe. On the other hand, she may be so torn by inner division, so victimized by a lack of faith, hope, and love, that she mars human prosperity negatively, by failing to do her share. To be persuasive to the female half of the race, future Christian theology will have to show how love of God like Jesus' should build effective characters.

Grollenberg hints at how to show this when he notes that Jesus seems to have put the "primal forces" that most of us use for self-defense at the service of other people. Because he left his self-defense to God, Jesus could be, in Bonhoeffer's phrase, "the man for others." In the case of women, both theology and general culture will have to work harder than has been their wont, if such self-defense or self-concern is to fall away energizingly.

Systematically, this may lead to Jesus' divine sonship, in contrast to his divine childhood. That is, Jesus' trust in his Abba may well have entailed a sexual self-affirmation. As son to Father, he may so have been affirming God that his own "manly" taking care, taking charge, being reliable and the like grew in each period of prayer. And while the Semitic culture of Jesus' day may well have allowed for more tender fathers and more resolute mothers than our own culture does, it seems likely that taking charge with vigor was more a male prerogative than a female one even in Jesus' time.

So, to achieve *her* proper golden mean, her love that radiates powerfully from a confident self to both God and neighbor, today's woman perhaps needs maternal rather than paternal imagery for God. This is the link to the Goddess that Carol Christ and other feminists have been making. When the ultimate power that runs the universe is symbolized in female terms, women gain a tremendous source of self-affirmation. If the Goddess is the way to express women's share in such ultimate power, Christian theology ought to open to the Goddess. How it can do this, as well as how it can open to other symbolizations of divinity, will concern us in the next section. Here we most need to underscore women's need to find Jesus' love invigorating, so that they, too, can leave debilitating self-concerns behind and get on with the work of liberating their whole culture.

Minimally, of course, the woman desiring this progress deserves the help of her community, its support for her virtuous growth. However, as many of the quotations I have made from today's male theologians show, even after some years of women's agitation for equal representation in language, the theological establishment has little sensitivity to the sexism of its ordinary speech. For most male theologians, I suspect, women are still so low on the horizon that theology can push its pen oblivious of their plight. A few men, though, protest that abandoning the generic "man" would sully their limpid style. Introducing "she" now and then in place of the generic "he" somehow sticks in their craw. "Fine," I think we should say, "Stick it in your craw. If you care so little for many women's sensitivities, you deserve to sputter and choke."[13]

FEMINIST REFLECTIONS II

This unladylike speech escapes my unpainted lips because I'm weary of male fatuousness about sexist language. The person to whom *America* sent my *Contemporary Catholic*

Theology for review called the work "oppressively feministic" because "One must tolerate the repetition of such phrases as 'God grants us her favor' and be open to the possibility of praying to 'Our Mother, who art in heaven.'"[14] Lost in that vast clerical tract where the sun don't shine, this reviewer exemplifies to almost comic perfection Rosemary Ruether's description of the public "freakout" so many church leaders enact when they meet a challenge to their identification of "God" with "male":

> Although it may not be true, in terms of strict theological tradition, that maleness can be literally ascribed to God or regarded as *essential* to the incarnation of God in Christ, operationally the psychic identification between these figures and male identity is very deep. So much so that when the very idea of severing the connection between the two is suggested, we witness, again and again, what amounts to a public "freak-out" by church leaders and teachers.[15]

Having noted that I am again speaking from personal experience, from the pain of having my own ox gored, the reader can enter whatever qualifications she thinks apt. Even after serious efforts to get this question of theological language into calm perspective, however, I remain amazed at the intransigence and stupidity of "conservatives" like my reviewer. Their psychic disturbance manifestly is so great that they lose all judgment about who their real enemies are. As a result, women hungry to bring their Christian faith alive, to make the millennial notion of the *imago Dei* significant for the female half of the race, meet with uncomprehension or even fury. Maleness (and, in the case of my Catholic tradition, clerical power) prove more important than the good of the faithful or the service of the Kingdom. In effect, Christian faith has become a personal fief (a male estate, a clerical privilege) rather than a ministry.

All the more reason, then, to attack the insistence on male language for the Christian God head-on. Dorothee Sölle, a strong political theologian, attacks by way of relativization (calling it a *minimum* demand):

> There are many examples of tentative attempts being made [to introduce new kinds of God-talk] everyplace where women have become aware of their situation. The desire for another way of imagining God, other symbols, other hopes is important for those who need another God because they are insulted, humiliated and repulsed by the culture in which we live. I believe relativization—giving up absolutist symbolization of God—represents a minimum demand.[16]

Sölle goes on to note that, besides father, we can call God mother, sister, fountainhead, spring of all goodness, living wind, and many other names. From the mystical tradition, she finds numerous examples that don't depend on sex or family relations at all. The feminist critique of God-talk therefore can blend into both traditional apophatic (negative) theology, which stressed God's distance from all this-worldly symbols,[17] and the impersonal predilection of the Eastern religions, wherein Brahman, Tao, and Buddhanature generally stand at some distance from the human psyche.

So, relativization comes to mean pluralism or diversity. Very many symbols apply to God usefully, if we employ them by the (quite traditional) canons of analogy. Ruether's reference to the "strict theological tradition" points up the ignorance that stalks too much discussion of God-talk, as well as its lack of mystagogy. In the strict theological and mystical traditions, God is more unlike than like our predication. To meet the living God we must enter a "cloud of unknowing," pass through a "dark night." Not a little of the purpose of these purgative passages is the removal of our wrongful humanization of God. For profound faith, we have to *realize,* not merely know notionally, that God is not *a* being, not another thing midst the world's play-pile. As Michael Buckley has recently shown, the projectionist theories of atheism (e.g., Feuerbach, Freud) and the traditional masters of mysticism (e.g., John of the Cross) agree in demanding such maturation.[18] Women therefore have fine precedents they can call upon when they present their case for the renovation of theological language.

In this context, we may be able partially to solve the dilemma that Jesus himself presents many Christian feminists. Hearing much validity in the charge that a male incarnation of divinity has made the male god, many Christians yet cling to the apostolic conviction that no one has ever spoken as Jesus did, that Jesus has nonpareil words of liberation. Were the Christian feminist able to relate to Jesus' God as father or mother, personal or impersonal source, she might feel her dilemma ease somewhat. Were she encouraged to make Jesus a leader and lover who wants her most lively, energetic faith, she might feel the dilemma largely melt away.

2/Psychology

CHAPTER THREE: THE FEMINIST SELF

Our several allusions to the "image of God," which has played a central part in traditional theological anthropology as well as in traditional controls on theological language, show that in moving to "psychology," the domain of the self, we shall retain many ties to theology, the domain of ultimate reality or divinity. The central theme in this chapter will be recent feminist reflections on the self, especially the liberated female self that is struggling to emerge. Before beginning this theme, however, we might do well to heed the conclusion of Carolyn Sherif's balanced chapter, "What Every Intelligent Person Should Know About Psychology and Women."[1] After reporting on the different trends emerging from the several contemporary psychological schools that have been studying women, Sherif draws a firm bottom line:

> What every intelligent person should know is that the "causes" of human experiences and actions are much more complex than any

> of the traditional schools of psychology we have reviewed: those that seek determinants within the individual to the neglect of the environment, that seek preordained determinants in a biology itself tainted with social myths, or that look for determinants only in the environment, as though the human individual were a passive empty shell (p. 178).

The psychological work that has received the most kudos in feminist circles probably is Dorothy Dinnerstein's *The Mermaid and the Minotaur.*[2] By using both Freudian and Gestalt perspectives, Dinnerstein avoids any simplemindedness about the deep and pervasive troubles that now beset the relations between the sexes. Still, she has a clear point of view, a laser-like focus on our current child-rearing. The manifold ambivalence that women and men now feel toward one another likely goes back to our earliest psychic formation. Women so dominate the formative time, when aboriginal loves and hates pulsate with almost volcanic intensity, that through the rest of life the female visage is for both women and men a blank check on which they can write almost any emotion:

> The deepest root of our acquiescence in the maiming and mutual imprisonment of men and women lies in a monolithic fact of human childhood: Under the arrangements that now prevail, a woman is the parental person who is every infant's first love, first witness, and first boss, the person who presides over the infant's first encounters with the natural surround and who exists for the infant as the first representative of the flesh (p. 28).

Other psychologists, of course, have stressed the importance of mother-child intimacy,[3] but few have done so with anything like Dinnerstein's insight into its causal relation to our social pathologies. These social pathologies run the gamut from macho bellicosity to female fluttering, with special emphasis on our lethal warmaking and ecological destructiveness. In a brilliant symbolic stroke, Dinnerstein summarizes the inhumanity our current sexual arrangements produce: they make us mermaids and minotaurs, monsters from a nightmarish mythology. The mermaid is the treacherous, seductive, impenetrable female swimming languorously in the dark waters from which life emerges. She lures male voyagers to their doom. The minotaur is the fearsome, gigantic, eternally infantile offspring of unnatural lust. He symbolizes male power as mindless, greedy, and insatiably devouring of human flesh.

Correlated with this teratology are the social roles men and women play. Men have seized a monopoly on making history. By and large, only they have been free to go to war, go to the laboratory, go on the political stump. Women have had to run the home and play the supporting roles. The result has been a peculiar differentiation in the sexes' expenditure of erotic energy: "Since it is he whose sexual impulsivity is legitimate, while she is expected to be receptive and undemanding, it is he, not she, at whose initiative erotic energy can with propriety be withdrawn from love and invested in worldly affairs: She, not he, is the one who must wait when the other turns away and be sexually available when he comes back" (p. 208).

"History" is Dinnerstein's shorthand for the whole world of affairs and culture. Women's exclusion from history has not only frustrated them enormously, causing much of their erotic energy to back up and turn brackish, it has also warped history itself, allowing uncomplemented male eros to make a world of excessive strife.

Pushing off from the female-dominated childhood they hold in common, adult males and females collude in creating what amount to mirror paths. Men enjoy the power of history-making, but they seek women's sanction and applause. Women resent their second-class citizenship, but they enjoy their exemption from history's hard knocks. This description admits of considerable qualification, of course, especially when one moves out of the Western middle and upper classes. Nonetheless, it puts a fine psychoanalytic point on both women's current protests and the current analysis of women's "sins." Deepening de Beauvoir's characterization of women's position as a socially sanctioned cowardice, Dinnerstein writes:

> The immunity life offers women is immunity not only from the risks and exertions of history-making, but also from the history-maker's legitimate internal misgivings about the value of what he spends his life doing. The use that both sexes make of this female immunity, their mutual motive in fostering it, is in my view the morbid core of our sexual arrangement. To uncover it is the main point of this book (p. 213).[4]

WOMEN'S SPIRITUAL QUEST

The main point of *this* book is to uncover the places where feminism and Christianity, taken as deep spiritual paths, converge. Toward this purpose, the recent feminist interest in what Carol Christ has called women's "spiritual quest" is especially germane. Christ's *Diving Deep and Surfacing*[5] deals with five feminist literary figures whose work depicts women's quest dramatically.

The five authors are Kate Chopin, Margaret Atwood, Doris Lessing, Adrienne Rich, and Ntozake Shange. Of the spiritual quest they share, Christ writes:

> Women's *spiritual quest* concerns a woman's awakening to the depths of her soul and her position in the universe. A woman's spiritual quest includes moments of solitary contemplation, but it is strengthened by being shared. It involves asking basic questions: Who am I? Why am I here? What is my place in the universe? In answering these questions, a woman must listen to her own voice and come to terms with her own experience. She must break long-standing habits of seeking approval, of trying to please parents, lovers, husbands, friends, children, but never herself. In probing her experience and asking basic questions, a woman may begin to wonder whether she has ever chosen anything she has done (pp. 8-9).

The personal preface to *Diving Deep and Surfacing* locates such probing and questioning in Christ's own autobiography. Long before writing her book, she felt that nature was where she might find the powers necessary to ground her life, and that male-dominated culture was simply inadequate to her needs and aspirations. The connection betwen these autobiographical feelings and her later study of feminist writers shone forth in an insight into *stories*. So long as they did not have their own stories, women could not name their distinctive experiences and discover themselves. The authors Christ studies therefore represent a stream important to the mass of the women's movement. In the pattern of discovery their heroines display, the authors have writ large what a great many contemporary women are undergoing. For Christ, this pattern entails an experience of nothingness (non-support), an insight, and a new naming. It is a sort of conversion process that moves from a sense of dis-ease, through a realization that change is necessary, to a fresh vision of the world. At the end, the woman feels akin to the first human beings, who named the creatures with whom they shared the earth and so felt a measure of control.

Kate Chopin's *The Awakening,* published in 1899, depicts a woman coming to understand her own creative needs but unable to withstand strong social opposition. Edna Pontellier realizes the injustice and pathos of her situation, but she can only change it by suicide. This drastic final measure leaves her story a highly ambiguous and cautionary tale. Insofar as Edna escaped social bondage, she gained a spiritual liberation. Insofar as society refused her a room of her own, she suffered a public defeat. By contrast, the heroine of Margaret Atwood's *Surfacing* wins through to a public victory. After her conversion, which takes the form of an intimacy with nature much like that which archaic women likely enjoyed, she is sufficiently her own person to contemplate a new, self-directed way of life. Christ underscores the importance of such a discovery of the powers nature offers: "By naming anew the great powers and women's grounding in them, such novels provide women with alternatives to patriarchal notions of power that can aid their struggle to change the social world" (p. 50).

Doris Lessing was the writer who first awakened Christ herself, especially through the culminating volume of her *Children of Violence* series, *The Four Gated City*. Martha Quest, the heroine of the series, is above all engaged in naming her experience, getting her alienation from the modern world clearly in sight. This takes her on a mystic journey to the edge of madness, where she must confront the destructive violence at the core of modern culture. Still, Martha discovers within herself powers to withstand such violence. Though Lessing's ideas about humanity's future may be overly apocalyptic, Christ finds her psychic insights a great feminist resource.

It is the poet Adrienne Rich, though, who has fashioned the vision Christ finds most adequate, especially concerning the integration of women's spiritual quest with a new social reality. Diving under the wreck of male culture, Rich searches for a new set of social relationships, based on women's reverence for life. In terms of black women's experience, Ntozake Shange expresses a similar search. Her "choreopoem" *For Colored Girls Who Have Considered Suicide When the Rainbow Is Enuf* portrays almost brutally the rape and psychological abuse to which black women have been subjected. When the chorus sing of finding god in themselves and loving her fiercely, we hear the thealogy that Christ's search for "grounding powers" has been implying. The term of Carol Christ's spiritual quest is the Goddess. She is the pearl of great price with which the woman who dives deep may hope to surface.

MORE RECENT LITERARY DEVELOPMENTS

The lesbian politics informing Rich's poetry, and the thealogy that emerges from Shange's exploration of the black ghetto,[6] both derive from the abusive character of male-dominated culture. So do the quest of Doris Lessing's early novels and the journey of Margaret Atwood's *Surfacing*. It seems fair, then, to characterize the main movement of Christ's literary figures as *away* from men. To find themselves, these figures' heroines have to lose their subjection to male-dominated culture. In Starhawk's terms, they need at least separation, if not separatism.

Perhaps it is significant, therefore, that the writing both Lessing and Atwood have done since the works that Christ treats seems to bring women back to men. Without retracting their criticisms of male-dominated culture, both authors now seem to deal with men more calmly, and to make greater provision for men's rehabilitation, as well as women's. To be sure, neither Lessing nor Atwood ever set up as a "feminist" author, a writer indentured to "women's" issues. Each rather worked as an artist who happened to be a woman, and who discovered that this happenstance made all the difference to her "reality."

As that reality has unfolded, however, sex seems to have changed from a major to a minor motif. In both artists' broader vision, it is not less vivid but less cramped. Atwood's novel *Life Before Man*[7] has no heroines or heroes. The three main characters, two women and one man, are equally deformed by secularist malaises. Doris Lessing's new (and magnum) opus, *Canopus in Argos: Archives,*[8] pays special attention to women's situations, but in the context of a massive imaginative effort to rework the entire foundation of Western culture.

The first volume of *Canopus in Argos* concentrates on Shikasta, the planet Earth sufficiently evolved for its pathology to have become blatant. Here is Lessing reflecting on the place of women in Western culture (note that she is also reflecting on *all* the servant classes):

> In Shikasta a race dominant in one epoch may be subservient in the next. A race of people in a condition of slavery in one time or place may within a few decades become master of others. The roles of the females have adjusted accordingly, and whenever a people, a country, a race, is *down,* then its females, doubly burdened, will be used as servants in the homes of the dominating ones.

> Such a female, often to the detriment of her own children, whom she may even have to abandon, may be the prop, the stay, the support, the nourishment of an entire family, and perhaps for all her life. For her *working* life, for such a servant may be turned out in old age without any more than what she came with. Yet she may have been the bond that held the family together.
>
> An unregarded if not despised person, someone at least considered inferior, and thought of not so much as an individual as a role—a *servant:* but this female in fact being the centre of a family, its point of balance—it is a situation that has been re-created over and over again, in every time, every culture, every place . . . (p. 151).

The second volume, *The Marriages Between Zones Three, Four, and Five,* has the fullest reflections on male-female relations. Indeed, the basic concern of the whole book is the balance of female-male qualities a healthy culture requires. Lessing goes so far as to portray as necessary a "fall" from the refinements, the intuitive and aesthetic perfections, of a female-dominated higher culture. The mysterious higher powers who command the destinies of the planet's different culture "zones" decree that Al·Ith, queen of the higher zone three, should marry king Ben Ata of the lower zone four. This queen, a marvel of feminine intelligence, is repelled by the brutish crudity of the soldier-king. Educating him away from his male chauvinism and violence proves a sore trial, but one with an unexpected twist. For, though the queen loses some of her refinement, becoming unable even to remember her pristine spiritual self, she gains an animal vitality. Lessing shows this through the couple's sexual relations, which descend from a subtle play to a fierce need.

ANDROGYNY

Queen Al·Ith's new carnal experiences produce in her a great sympathy for the passions that rule the unrefined peoples outside zone three. From another point of view, they are the price for Ben Ata's education to a greater refinement.

One sees, then, a certain convergence. Exquisite feminine sensibility moves "down" toward crude masculine carnality, while crude masculine carnality moves "up" toward exquisite feminine sensibility. Indeed, in the novel's later passages Ben Ata plays the "superior" to an "inferior" queen of zone five, whose people are even more savage than the citizens of his military regime. "Level after level," Lessing says. "Wheels within wheels." The permutations of body-based vigor and spirit-based refinement are almost limitless.

We glimpse the rationale for Al·Ith's assignment to Ben Ata, and a philosophy capable of embracing the many permutations of flesh and spirit, in volume three, *The Sirian Experiments.* Probably the major thesis of volume three is that a *necessity* guides the cosmos, and that those who dictate a planet's fate do so in the service of this necessity. Ambien II, the female high-ranking representative of Sirius who narrates volume three, passes through what amounts to an initiation, so that she may better appreciate this necessity. The necessity manifests itself through moral laws, whose breaking leads to natural and cultural disorder. In the following dialogues with a male representative of Canopus, a superior planet, Ambien II stretches to the point where she almost grasps both the cosmic necessity and the trust it demands:

> "You announce these laws to me with such authority!" "Canopus did not invent the Laws. Have you not observed for yourself that if one disconnects oneself from a process arbitrarily, then all kinds of connections and links and growths are broken—and that you yourself suffer for it?" "Very well, then—yes, as you speak, it seems that I do remember seeing this myself. Very often when you say things of this kind, I might object or deny or refuse—and then later, on reflection, I see the truth of what you say. But I can only repeat that I do not decide Colonial policy," and I asked, "Who is it above *you,* then, that makes laws?" And he laughed at this. "Laws are not *made*—they are inherent in the nature of the Galaxy, of the Universe." "You are saying that we have to learn how to observe these laws in operation?" "Yes, Sirius, yes, yes" (p. 240).

The discussion then becomes practical, for Canopus wants Sirius to take up an apparently bootless task, on no basis, finally, but trust:

> "You want me to go back and try and persuade Sirius to take responsibility for the Southern Continents again?" "Yes, we do." "Although our rule is so much less effective than yours? Although we, Sirius, cannot give to a situation what you can give?" He said gently, with a diffidence that was rooted in his nature, and that I have seen very seldom in my career: "If you will consent to act with us, so that we can influence through you, then perhaps things can at least be ameliorated. Maintained. Prevented from getting worse." "Why, why, *why?* What is the purpose of your concern?" "Sometimes we have to take things on trust!" "Are *you* taking things on trust?" "Do you imagine it could be otherwise? Sirius, this Galaxy is vast, is infinitely various, is always changing, is always beyond what we can see of it, in whatever little corner is our home." "To hear you call Canopus a little corner is—not easy to understand. Can it possibly be that just as I watch *you,* Canopus, while I strive and strive to understand—because I have to admit this, though of course you know it already!—is it possible that just as this is my relation to you, then so is your relation to—to . . ." and my mind faded out, into its depths (p. 241).

Once again, then, level upon level. A major lesson I read in the *Canopus in Argos: Chronicles* that has appeared to date (more volumes are promised) is the need to balance activity with passivity, strong effort to change unjust situations with rational surrender to the concatenated mystery of a cosmos much larger than human intelligence. The link between these two attitudes is an active-passive discernment of the laws according to which the cosmos runs. However, we earthly readers so strongly identify with Ambien II's difficulty in rising to the level of these laws that Canopus's counsel to trust is no passing matter.

Taken *en gros,* the three volumes express what I would call an impersonal androgyny. Lessing deals with personal qualities, and she writes shrewd psychologies of both men and women. But the overall effect is (1) to show the complementarity of these psychologies, the mutual need "feminine" and "masculine" traits have for one another, and (2) to subordinate the psychologies to that deep openness we have simply as human beings, below our differentiation into men and women.

I do not mean Lessing would deny that sex colors all our perceptions, nor do I mean that her "androgyny" (which is my term, not hers) is that uncritical melding of qualities to which many feminists rightly object. I mean rather that she takes the full range of human characteristics into account, and that the sex of the contemplative whose initiation volume three describes matters less than her attunement to a higher order, to the music of the spheres. Ambien II's tutor from Canopus is a male, but in his higher culture, metempsychosis (transmigration of souls) is a way of life, and his different incarnations take him to male and female bodies almost indiscriminately. Far more important than his sex in any of his incarnations is his intuitive sense of *the way things are.* He is the closest thing to a futuristic Taoist one could want.

CHRISTIAN REFLECTIONS I

One wanting a futuristic feminist (anonymous) Christian could do much worse than Klorathy, the tutor from Canopus. Ambien II, for that matter, is an admirable character. Much of the attractiveness of both lies in their realism. They try mightily to understand the world in which they live, to go with the world's flow rather than against it. As a result, they give the world's variety, the world's heterogeneity, its due. I would make this realism a *sine qua non* for future Christian feminism. Emerging from the Christian ghetto, it ought to acknowledge, indeed to embrace, the prodigal variety of humanity's ways to God. It also ought to embrace the insights and problems of men, who continue to be just less than half the race.

It is its neglect of this realism that disqualifies radical lesbianism in my view. No doubt, the fact that I am heterosexual and happily married (without children) limits my ability to understand the radical lesbian position. On the other hand, I have no difficulty with lesbianism as such, believing that its benefits for many women are incontrovertible. Were we to place this discussion in terms of Canopus's acceptance of the cosmic laws, I would nominate homosexuality as one of the empirical, *de facto* patterns that the Christian realist embraces. My problem is only with the ("radical") position that calls for separatism (a life apart from men) and the denigration of most things male.

Perhaps a simple look at some statistics will explain why I call this radical position unrealistic. If women are 51 percent of the population, and the population is about 10 percent homosexual, then about 5 percent of the population is lesbian. My experience is that not one in five of the lesbians I know is separatist, which means that a generous accounting would give the radical lesbian position a constituency of about 2 percent. The way I understand theology, philosophy, ethics, and other ventures in describing reality and prescribing human action, a position is disqualified almost immediately when one discovers that it serves only a fraction of the population. That is why I cannot take the misanthropic "meta-ethics" of a Mary Daly seriously.

Mary Daly will return, to receive a fuller hearing, below. My point here is facing the implications of Doris Lessing's realism. Fortunately, a similar realism about men, although perhaps without Lessing's distanced objectivity, occurs in numerous feminist works today. For example, Madonna Kolbenschlag's *Kiss Sleeping Beauty Good-Bye*[9] concludes with a letter to men (the "Frog Prince") that makes her concern for men's liberation obvious. The Frog Prince has to take a few good raps on the chin, but Sleeping Beauty and the other fairy-tale feminists are compassionate toward his problems.

Thus, they tell the Prince: "In many ways, you are more fragile than I. I know if I leave you, it will crush you beyond anything I suffer. By being a good wife, mother, mistress, servant, handmaid, Girl Friday—and little else—I've made you all the more dependent on me for your sense of well-being. The impression of autonomy that you project to others is a well-practiced reflex. But you are not a truly free person" (p. 210). Again:

> As a conditioned male you must undergo a mutilation of spirit that amputates some of your deepest human capacities. Feelings are perhaps the most serious threat to the masculine ideal. You are expected to play the role of the independent strong achiever, always in control, always deliberate, calculated. You are expected to be task-oriented, undistracted by personal matters. You are expected to repress any responses that might impede your efficiency in achieving your goals. And so you listen neither to your feelings, nor to your body (p. 211).

There is little in these quotations to quarrel with, and yet I cannot grade them A+. Lessing's Ben Ata fits the quotations to a *T,* but his interaction with Al·Ith is a more realistic "duel," because his strengths also are clear. On the other side of our feminist dissection laboratories, across from where we work on the mermaids and minotaurs, we need more attention to healthy human beings, male as well as female. Otherwise, we forget that Sleeping Beauty and the Frog Prince are fairy tales.

At the very beginning of her work, Kolbenschlag writes: "This book concerns itself with the obstacles to self-actualization, transcendence, and redemption that constitute the challenge of being female—and at the same time, of being fully human—in the contemporary era. If it has any uniqueness in the chorus of voices that have already spoken on the subject, it is that this work assumes the perspective of faith" (p. xiii). The letter to the Frog Prince is a sensitive adieu but not an explicitly Christian *a Dieu.* In my view, Christian feminists do less than their full job until they make the personal and social sides of the feminist movement crackle with Jesus' parabolic fire. Kolbenschlag provides for

Jesus, but she does not sear the Prince with the new love of the Kingdom. The Prince should hear that he must repent his foolish ways, must believe in the good news of immortalizing divine life. He should hear that all things are possible with God, even men's and women's joint dwindling to insignificance before the consuming necessity of the Spirit.

CHRISTIAN REFLECTIONS II

Recent studies of the life cycle have made many of us more sensitive to the self's typical developmental crises. Erik Erikson has done the pioneer work in this field, but feminists seem, at best, guarded in their judgments about his conclusions. Thus, quoting Gail Sheehy,[10] Kolbenschlag implies that Erikson's "generativity" does not fit the situation of most mature women (p. 25). As in the case of Erikson's notion of women's "inner space,"[11] this implication seems to derive, in large part, from an ideological opposition to any man's pronouncing on women's condition.

To be sure, psychology has been no more androgynous, in the praiseworthy sense I applied to Lessing, than Christian theology has been. Both disciplines, on the whole, have considered male experience normative. Both, on the whole, have been like the Mishnah, viewing woman as an anomaly.[12] The notion of women's inner space is liable to applications that make anatomy destiny. The notion of generativity can reflect such a male bias that women's frequently different timetables little impinge on the discussion. On the other hand, both inner space and generativity can greatly illumine the psychology of women. If given a chance, treated sympathetically, they can shed considerable light on the stereotypic-yet-real orientation women have toward nurturing.

My interest in this section is a Christian reflection on women's life cycle, so I shall lay "inner space" to the side. The major virtues that Erikson's life-cycle scheme postulates for the mature personality are care and wisdom. "Care" is "the widening concern for what has been generated by love, necessity, or accident; it overcomes the ambivalence arising from irreversible obligation." Wisdom is "the detached and yet active concern with life itself in the face of death itself . . . it maintains and conveys the integrity of experience, in spite of the decline of bodily and mental functions."[13] I see nothing in this description of wisdom that disqualifies it as the strength women most need in old age. To rehabilitate care, which suffers abuse more easily, one need only pay attention to the epigenetic conflict from which care issues (when the conflict is successfully resolved).

As wisdom is the virtue required in old age, so care is the virtue required in what Erikson calls "maturity." Maturity follows on young adulthood, when human beings typically resolve the conflict between intimacy and isolation to produce the virtue of love. In maturity, the self's psychological clock ticks away at the problem of love's fruits. Will the person who is now relatively complete, relatively well equipped for productivity, become generative, or will s/he be self-absorbed? For Erikson, the "victory" of generativity over self-absorption results in care. As is the case with all life-cycle victories, one is dealing with a relative preponderance, not a rout that chases the "negative" possibility from the field. A certain amount of self-absorption remains, to some extent because it is useful and necessary. But the greater stress in maturity should be on generativity, for the sake both of the individual and of society. The individual needs to be needed. Society needs good workers and caretakers. Especially, the younger generation needs mature people to teach, minister, heal, and lead it. Without such mature people, the generations become unhinged and society unravels.

Now, the feminist problem with Eriksonian care roots in a valid observation. Many women spend the years from their late teens to menopause caring for children and men. Slowly, they build the fires of a great need for *self*-development, and so interpreting maturity as a time for self-sacrifice can fit their epigenesis badly. However, were one to stress the generative thrust behind care, and to note how broadly Erikson understands generativity, most of the problem would become semantic. Generativity is more than "feminine" nurturing. It is also "masculine" productivity, creativity, drive for success. Androgynizing generativity, one could easily understand care to be more than self-sacrifice for children or master-husbands. It is for culture, social service, and public events as well. The generative person is expressing a need to be needed, a need to use her time well. Whether through child-rearing or painting, nursing or engineering, the inner daimons urge her to "husband" her time, so that it may bear rich increase.

At this point, the Christian ought to call to mind the Johannine stress on fruitfulness (John 15), not neglecting the submotif of the pruning that fruitfulness may require. What has to be pruned? Self-absorption that gets in the way of ministry *(diakonia)*. The Christian has a charge to love neighbor as self. Care and generativity are psychological correlatives to this charge. We can't love our neighbors well if we love ourselves deficiently, but we also can't love our neighbors well if we love ourselves excessively. The wisdom to know the difference may only become clear when the advent of death strips away the illusions most of us indulge in, but we can strive for wisdom long before we become feeble.

The advent of death, I take it, is the time in the life cycle when the larger issues of life step forth in greater clarity. Then one becomes like Lessing's Canopians, concerned to see things in the round, *sub specie aeternitatis.* Then men and women, equally mortal, have to ask themselves what temporal things really matter. If wisdom is the ability to love life in the face of death, to maintain integrity in the face of dissolution, generativity and care are wisdom's propaedeutic. By finding her own way to use time well, to be productive, the Christian woman bears fruit abundantly. Then, when death imperils even this fruit, she has to face the Mystery of creativity unblinkingly, has to realize in her fragile bones how God is the crux of life's meaning. If there is no creative power greater than her own, no love that is immortal, she is of all women the most to be pitied. On the other hand, if Christ has been a truth-teller, if the resurrection is real poetry, she may be of all women the most filled with joy.[14]

CHAPTER FOUR: CHRISTIAN SELFHOOD

As Christian feminists ponder the therapies their tradition needs, the deeper among them strive to fill all of women's lives with a biblical joy. Thus, the deeper among them call for a thorough recasting of the Christian world-view, so that, theologically, psychologically, sociologically, and ecologically, the needs of the whole human species, male and female, can receive their due. On the way to this better world-view, many Christian feminists feel they have to go backwards in order to advance. That is, they feel a need to retrieve women's past experience and leadership, under the shrewd suspicion that most history-writing hitherto has hewed to a male main-line. Rosemary Ruether and Eleanor McLaughlin's *Women of Spirit*[1] is a good effort in this direction. As its chapters show, there have been innumerable Christian women who have outwitted the male-dominated system. Refusing to hide their light under a bushel, these women have used charismatic authority to force the body ecclesiastic to listen to their contributions.

The rationale for historical retrieval such as Ruether and McLaughlin's is admirably clear from their Introduction: "In this collection of essays on leadership roles of women in the Jewish and Christian traditions, we hope to make a contribution both toward the recovery of important chapters of women's history and toward the charting of the paradigms of female leadership possible within successive theological world views. These are both difficult problems" (p. 16). True enough. Not only have most of the past histories been devoted to male thinking and doing, but also many of the women in past epochs have internalized patriarchal ideologies, fitting their self-images to the models the male establishment proposed.

Nonetheless, careful scholarship seems capable of hauling many strong women up in its net. Some of them are marginals, operating outside the system. But others are women who turned the tradition's ideals against its contemporary practice. Impressed by these latter foremothers, Ruether and McLaughlin question the wisdom of feminist research that ignores the mainstream: "in our opinion much of this search is mistaken. . . . Important women do appear as leaders in marginal movements, but they are not more important than women leaders who arise at the center" (p. 19).

There is good work on women's spirituality today that continues this orthodox tradition.[2] Perforce, it tends to come from feminists with good academic training, who are both sensitive to present women's needs and equipped with the tools of critical historical research. In keeping with feminism's egalitarian aspirations, however, the Christian spiritual theologian would also do well to study the faith of the female *hoi polloi,* noting, beneath the apparent conservatism or even fundamentalism of many church women, the creative reinterpretations of the received tradition that allow many "ordinary" women to go on.

Sometimes the best indications of this populist creativity come obliquely, through studies that are not explicitly theological. For example, the five women who dominate Robert and Jane Hallowell Coles' *Women of Crisis*[3] all recognize a faith dimension in their struggles. Thus the first pages of the story of Hannah, an Appalachian woman, sketch a context of faith: "'I believe that on my deathbed, when my soul is leaving my body and preparing to meet God, I will be having one of those dreams I've had, on and off, all my life. I do believe that.' She always added that shorter, four-word affirmation . . ." (p. 73). The woman, transplanted from the hills of Harlan County, eastern Kentucky, to Dayton, Ohio, is traditional in believing that her soul will be judged by God. But she is creative and rebellious in her dreams, which express a desire for liberation as passionate as that of any card-carrying feminist.

Hannah's dreams were nurtured by her grandmother:

> When I was a little girl, my grandmother took me aside and said she wanted to tell me something important, and I must never forget what she would say. She practically whispered her story to me—that I was a girl and not a boy, and a girl should pay attention to the colors of leaves in the autumn, while boys just ran all over them and didn't see what was there on the ground before them: yellow and red and green and orange brown, a rainbow of colors, God's love spread out before us to feast on (p. 84).

So, in middle age, Hannah trudges along, accepting the drudgery of her work as a supermarket cashier. In her dreams, though, she hopes mightily: for a better job, a better future for her daughter, and a better love from her husband. All these, she knows, God desires for her, since salvation surely means a freer, better life. Hannah's dreams are contemplations of God's justice.

CONTEMPLATION

Freud has left us the wise observation that human health entails the capacities to love and to work. Feminist literature is replete with analyses of love, especially sexual love, and analyses of women's work also abound. The Christian probably has to extend Freud's dyad in two directions. In addition to the capacities to love and to work, human health, as Christian faith sees it, involves the capacities to contemplate and to advance politics. The Christian self prays and labors for justice. Here my topic is Christian contemplative prayer, which I offer as a primary resource for a healthy psyche. Such contemplation is almost beyond the pale of secular feminism, likely to stir little more than a frown, and it is different from the power-raising exercises of the new witches. Thus, it can give Christian feminism a distinctive hue.

Certainly one of the reasons I applaud the Appalachian woman Hannah, and the other women of *Women of Crisis,* is that they *ponder* their experience. Though they seldom have much formal education, these women are deep. Whether they realize it or not, they are en route to wisdom, a view of the whole, of the end of things. A simple black maid from New Orleans, who appears in Robert Coles' *The Children of Crisis, V,*[4] speaks of "the end of things," and of the fate likely to befall the introspective little white girl for whom she cares: "She wonders about life, and what its about, and what the end of things will be. That's good. But she's stopping now, that's what they want: no looking, no staring, no peeking at life. No questions; they don't want questions. They go to a church a couple times a year, Christmas and Easter, and no one asks them any questions there. No one asks them questions anyplace they go" (p. 553).

Doris Lessing's narrator in *The Sirian Experiments* is a sister to this black maid, for she, too, ponders her experience. Indeed, since time immemorial, a rhythm of experience and reflection has furnished humanity its basic spirituality. Wise people have been those who profited from their experiences, who did not make the same mistake twice. Stupid people have been those who did not ponder and so profited hardly at all. One scarcely knows where to place the people of the modern university, whose catalogues make no provision for personal pondering. Perhaps they would be most at home with the Psalmist's fool, the one who says in his heart there is no Mystery worth contemplating.

Women have frequently distinguished themselves in the history of Christian contemplation, so the historical retrieval that Christian feminists are undertaking, along with the new hagiography sensitive to women's needs,[5] may give us doctors of spiritual theology other than Teresa of Avila. Were they to write with today's cadences, they probably would find much to approve in the simplified prayer being taught by those who have come under the influence of *The Cloud of Unknowing,* an anonymous fourteenth-century English classic. William Johnston, for example, has used his studies in *The Cloud,* along with his studies in modern literature and Zen Buddhism, to delineate the mystical core of a healthy religion.[6]

The mystical core of a healthy religion is simply love. Regarding prayer, it is an abiding with God as God in a spirit of heart-to-heart colloquy. When the contemplative is well instructed, she knows that God as God, the living divinity, is sure to cloud her mind. There is no way a finite mind can grasp an infinite reality clearly. So, there must be an "unknowing" of her false notions of God, an obnubilation that puts discursive reason in the shade. The purpose of this unknowing is not to evacuate the mind, so that the emotions may sing and dance. The purpose is to focus from the "heart," the center of the personality. From the heart, a finite person can commune with an infinite reality. She can take the "restlessness" of which Augustine spoke, the desire for "beatific vision" of which Aquinas spoke, and center it peacefully in the divine darkness. The author of *The Cloud* knew of no more salutary exercise. In his or her view, the flame of love that flickered in the divine darkness was precisely what might cleanse the personality in its depths, what might anneal it to strength, so that it could bear the divine embrace.

For Eastern Christianity, the teaching of *The Cloud* is bound to conjure the Jesus Prayer. The spiritual masters who continue to teach the Jesus Prayer today, including Mother Alexandra, the *hegumena* (superior) of the Monastery of the Holy Transfiguration in western Pennsylvania, make it clear that heart-to-heart love, core-to-core being-with, is the essence of Christian contemplation.[7] Under their repeated "Lord Jesus Christ, Son of the living God, have mercy on me, a sinner," thousands of orthodox Christians have actualized the Pauline profession, "I live, now not I, but Christ lives in me" (Gal. 2:20). Through their rosaries and Bible readings, many Catholic and Protestant Christians have communed with God similarly. In these ways, they have experienced the peace, joy, cleansing, and challenge of divine *agape.*

In my view, the "Christianization" of the ordinary contemplation involved in common-sense pondering, in deep thoughts late in the night, simply involves turning them toward the dark Mystery of "It All" and resting wordlessly, thoughtlessly, with a peaceful effort to love. The rest is expectant: the Mystery may draw near. The effort to love is in the spirit of Eriksonian wisdom and Canopian necessity: saying yes to what is, despite all the world's imperfections; saying yes to one's self, despite all one's regrets.

WORK

This yea-saying to the world and the self, this acceptance of necessity in trust, is a substantial portion of life's passion. The world and the self are "things" we have to undergo, to suffer, even more than they are things we have to change. If abused, this insight can lead to religions such as the Western religion Marx described: opium to dull the pain of the downtrodden. If neglected, however, this insight can lead to the Marxist impasse: what does one do when history proves intractable? Where does meaning reside, when the individual's life does not bring the classless society, the utopia, significantly closer? Unless we can accept the world and the self, suffering their imperfections by letting them repose in mystery, we cannot escape the plight of Sisyphus. Then, decade after decade, humanity keeps pushing its ambitions up history's hill, only to have them come crashing down again.

The Benedictine contemplative life coupled such warrants for prayer with a mandate to work. *Ora et labora* distilled the complete monastic routine. And the copula was not merely perfunctory, for work and prayer were to flow in and out of one another, making a systole and diastole. A major reason Western work has come on hard times is our culture's having broken work's connection to prayer. Without prayer as a counterbalance, Western work grows cancerous, having few of the cellular limits that make for health. At one extreme this produces workaholics, high-pressure types who fill the actuarial columns with early coronaries. At another extreme it produces slightly maniacal types who "play as hard as they work," riding their mechanical bulls, Winnebago campers, or pickups from the singles' bars into oblivion.

We will not change this pathological work by equalizing women's share in it. Statistical studies of women's economic segregation, however illuminating, bear little philosophic therapy.[8] No, we must deal with work more simply and humanely, listening to the core lament in so many workers' stories. One of Studs Terkel's interviewees spoke for a whole corps when she ruminated sadly, "I think most of us are looking for a calling, not a job. Most of us, like the assembly line worker, have jobs that are too small for our spirit. Jobs are not big enough for people."[9] But to look for a "calling" is to ask work to be a vocation. And to ponder who does such calling, where vocations come from, is to think in Hasidic terms, toward a "Master of the Universe."

When the Reformation attacked the notion of a two-level church, separated into clergy and laity, it fought to extend the Christian vocation to all the faithful. Laity, too, had a calling, and crafts persons' cottages might be as dignified as parsonages. Much of it is a question of how we regard our work, how we think of our working-time. If we regard our work as interwoven with our prayer, so that both our action and our contemplation are serving the twofold command, we will not experience work as so sundering, and we will not need a play that is merely abusive, mind-drugging "fun."

Zen Buddhism, which demands a most exacting meditation, makes the correlation between work and contemplation in terms of selflessness. As the Buddhist's meditation *(zazen)* is to actualize in her the truths of selflessness *(anatman),* so her work is to suffer none of the alienations that self-concern develops. Paradoxically, this selflessness emerges as salvation and self-realization:

> Questioner: What do you mean by "salvation"? Roshi: Liberation from the bind of ego, from the deluded notion of a

> separate reality called "I." From the Zen viewpoint, then, work has a far deeper purpose than simply turning out a product or rendering a service useful to society. Rightly regarded, it is a vehicle for Self-realization. But if work is to serve that function, workers must train themselves not to evaluate their jobs as boring or enjoyable, for one can only make such judgments by "stepping back," thus separating himself from his work. They must also learn to relate to their jobs singlemindedly, with nothing held back—in other words, with no "thought gaps" between themselves and their work. Performed this way, work acts as a cleanser, flushing away random, irrelevant thoughts, which are as polluting to the mind as physical contaminants are to the body. Thus work becomes an expression of True-mind, creative and energizing. This is the true nobility of labor. To work this way is called in Zen working for oneself.[10]

One thinks of Chuang Tzu's master carver, at one with his blade.[11] One thinks of Michael Polanyi's analysis of skills and tools.[12] In different ways they clarify the same goal: a worker who is an artist, a work in which worker and tools become one. E. F. Schumacher developed his "Buddhist Economics" by pondering Burmese insights along this line: "The Buddhist point of view takes the function of work to be at least threefold: to give a man a chance to utilise and develop his faculties; to enable him to overcome his ego-centredness by joining with other people in a common task; and to bring forth the goods and services needed for a becoming existence."[13] Christianity and feminism could forge a mighty union simply by agreeing on this anti-capitalist vision of labor.

FELICITAS TAYLOR

We shall come to Christian views of social justice in the next chapter, where I hope to buttress the implication that the gospel supports neither a Marxist nor a capitalist view of work. Much like Buddhist economics, Christian economics subordinates financial gain to such higher goods as the workers' self-development and the work's service of society's real needs. Few things better show the un-Christian character of current Western society than its obsession with financial profit. I was gratified in May, 1981, to learn that one of the many evangelical television shows Kansas receives was planning to devote more time to economic analyses and money-making, for that confirmed my impression that such evangelicals know virtually nothing about a genuinely Christian ethic.

E. F. Schumacher does know something about a genuinely Christian ethic:

> I think you are put into this life with the task of learning to distinguish between that which is really real and really important and permanent and of true value on the one hand, and things trivial, amusing, ephemeral, and of no real value on the other. Your intellect has to make that distinction. The world has to attach itself to the things that really matter and not to those ephemeral trivialities which make the most noise. That is the message of religion. I know it is normally handed down in all sorts of other ways, but unless you do that you are an unhappy, messed-up person.[14]

Any useful consideration of the self attempts, through its reflections on work, prayer, love, and the self's other main occupations, to illumine the causes of unhappiness and lessen the number of messed-up persons. Among the messed-up protagonists of recent feminist literature, Felicitas Taylor, the heroine of Mary Gordon's *The Company of Women,*[15] stands out. Felicitas is a young woman of considerable gifts. Despite a somewhat bizarre upbringing in the midst of a totally female circle dominated by a fiercely conservative Catholic priest, she becomes an intellectual with a heart that's a lonely hunter. I like Felicitas. The reflections Gordon puts in her mouth are deep and well worth pondering, especially for those who would probe the Christian self. Hear, then, some of Felicitas's thoughts at the end of the novel, when she has borne an illegitimate child, watched the child flower among the (now old) women, and is at the threshold of marriage to Leo, a quiet, unintellectual man:

"I am marrying him partly for silence. God knows there have been silences enough in the houses we have built here on this property, but they have been female silences, dreamy or murderous, or the menacing silence of the one man here [Cyprian, the priest]. Leo's is the silence of a man who finds the physical world truly absorbing. It is the only male silence that isn't dangerous" (p. 243). Hitherto, Felicitas has not found the physical world so absorbing as the intellectual. Cyprian trained her to regard an absorption with nature as an American heresy, an un-Christian pantheism. The physical shock of pregnancy, however, has disposed her to respect Leo's naturalism. In my terms, it has disposed her to ecology. She is not a good candidate for the new witchcraft, but she is on the verge of a sane reverence for creation.

Though she chooses marriage with Leo, Felicitas is not romantic. She marries for her child's sake, and to keep herself from the cruelty celibacy can develop:

> I fear the consequences of exposure, the toughening of my spirit, the silences of my own heart. And I fear in myself a growing cruelty of judgment I hope sex will keep me from. I have never understood random sexual desire. I like having Leo's arms around me; I enjoy being kissed. But the ardor I seem to inspire in him astounds me. I like to think that I am fond of sex. I'm proud of the pleasure I seem able to bring someone I care for. But sex really interests me only when it's over, when Leo is silent again, when I can feel the beating of his tired heart. The excitement, the high dramatic moments, all seem predictable to me. It is the intimacy I like . . ." (p. 260).

Though she wonders about her involvement with a man of so little mind, Felicitas wants to share life with him, because it could make her more human. The intimacy of sex, and all the other intimacies that crochet a marital union, hold out the prospect of a greater humanity, a better self. That seems to me a high marital ethics: sharing life to make better selves.

Gordon turns Felicitas's final reflections toward God, showing the scars Cyprian's tutelage has left:

> I am interested in the perception of the sacred. So many humans seem to hunger for it: the clear, the unencumbered. I too hunger, but my hunger is specific. If I could see the face of God as free from all necessity, the vision as the reward of a grueling search, the soul stripped down, rock hard, then I would look for Him. The pure light that enlightens every man. If He would show Himself so, then I would seek Him. But I will not let Him into my heart (pp. 264-65).

Felicitas is so hungry for specific human loves that she cannot let the divine light be but a modality of the divine love. She has miles to go before she sleeps, but she is an attractive pilgrim, honest and resolute.

FEMINIST REFLECTIONS I

Mary Daly is a resolute pilgrim, who has moved from Christianity to radical feminism. Her book *Gyn/Ecology: The Metaethics of Radical Feminism*[16] contains some of the sharpest criticism of Christianity on the current scene. Concerning our present topic, Daly charges Christianity with trying to murder the Goddess, the ultimate aura of the female self:

> The torture and burning of women as witches became normal and indeed normative in "Renaissance" Europe. The male members of the Mystical Body, attempting to act out the resurrection myth of their symbolic Head, strove for "re-birth" through Goddess-murder, that is, through the violent elimination of Female Presence. Their theology and their law required this massacre. Even to defend a witch was tantamount to declaring oneself a witch (p. 201).

The witch-hunts of the late medieval and early modern Christian times made those among the darkest periods of Church history. Daly argues that the witch-hunts expressed a misogynism inherent in Christianity. That she finds parallel misogynisms in Hindu widow-burning, African genital mutilation, and Chinese footbinding does little to alleviate this charge. Those who wish to understand the anger of many feminists, and to see the depths of the reform that Christian faith and practice require, will do well to attend to some of Daly's documentation.

For example, the *Malleus Maleficarium,* a catechism of demonology published in 1486, leveled the following broadside against women: "All witchcraft comes from carnal lust which is in women insatiable" (p. 180). Powered by this sort of prurient psychology, many of the inquisitors who hunted witches could justify unspeakable cruelties as punishment befitting agents of Satan. Thus a young woman accused of witchcraft in Germany in 1600 suffered the following all-too-typical tortures:

> she was hoisted repeatedly in the strappado (defined in Merriam-Webster as a torture consisting of "hoisting the subject by a rope sometimes fastened to his [sic] wrists behind his back and letting him fall to the length of the rope") . . . she bore this heroically, confessing nothing and pardoning those who had falsely accused her, even though she had been hoisted eleven times, ten of them with a fifty-pound weight. Ten weeks later she was hoisted again and was told that her mother had accused her, and then "her courage gave way" (p. 181).

The woman made an unsuccessful attempt at suicide, and then "confessed" to such crimes as having had intercourse with the devil from the age of eight, having killed many children (thirty of whose hearts she ate), having killed old people, raised tempests, killed cattle, renounced God, and so on.

The defense of the tortures that produced such confessions ran along the following lines: witchcraft is a special crime demanding special measures. For Jean Bodin, an eminent sixteenth-century intellectual, witchcraft directly assaulted the majesty of God, so it was fitting (for the good of the state) to appease God's wrath by special penalties. In Bodin's own horrifying logic: "one accused of being a witch ought never to be fully acquitted and set free unless the calumny of the accuser is clearer than the sun, inasmuch as the proof of such crimes is so obscure and so difficult that not one witch in a million would be accused or punished if the procedure were governed by ordinary rules" (p. 182).

According to Daly's sources, the number of women killed as witches might go well over nine million. She sees the general intent of the craze as "to break down and destroy strong women, to dis-member and to kill the Goddess, the divine spark of be-ing in women" (p. 183). As hinted earlier, I find Daly's overall philosophy impossible to accept, because it veers toward a blanket condemnation of men. In my view, the combination of her personal grievances and her feminist studies has caused her to lose hold of the objective order. In the objective order, men are a reality that is not going to go away, not all men are evil, the evils against women are not the only evils of history, and no philosophy or politics that withdraws from facts such as these deserves a fully serious hearing. Still, I wish Christian history were less replete with the abuses of women, gross and subtle, that make Daly's charge of a core misogynism somewhat plausible.

For, the female self has long found that Christianity considers her inferior to the male, and she has long had to battle for respect. From patristic times to the present, woman has been the weaker sex, the temptress to sin, the distaff side of an essentially male enterprise.[17] To this day, Roman Catholicism and Eastern Orthodoxy exclude women from orders, rendering those churches' ministries incredible to serious feminists. By the same statistical argument that casts separatist lesbianism in the shade, I find my Roman Catholic tradition's power-structure hopelessly incredible.

Limiting ordination to males with the charism for celibacy, it says that perhaps 5 percent of the population qualify for sacramental ministry and juridical church office. So much for the Vatican II ecclesiology of "The People of God." The men in charge prefer the preservation of their own power to a Church of equal opportunity, dignity for women, and leadership based on merit.

FEMINIST REFLECTIONS II

The historical and psychological forces that have caused almost all the Christian churches to treat women as second-class citizens are complex, but anti-traditional feminists are correct in attributing a great influence to popular Christianity's having projected an exclusively male God and savior. Neither Jesus' Abba nor Jesus himself need have become a sponsor of male supremacy, but the Church's abuse of both God the Father and God the Son has made them such. As a result, all but the most sophisticated Christians have found it "natural" that "the head of every woman is her husband" (I Cor. 11:3).

Naomi Goldenberg, who is not sophisticated in Christian theology but is sophisticated in religious psychology, has probed the "logic" of this male supremacy in the case of Pope Paul VI's ban on women priests:

> Conservative leaders of contemporary religious institutions understand that allowing women access to top positions of authority threatens the age-old composition of the institutions themselves. In January, 1977, Pope Paul VI issued a declaration affirming the Vatican's ban on allowing women to be ordained as Catholic priests. The document states that because Christ was a man and because he chose only male disciples, women can never serve as chief officials in the Catholic hierarchy.[18]

Goldenberg sees this position as stemming from a shrewd understanding of how symbols shape human consciousness.

For Paul VI, the priest had to be of the same sex as Christ because otherwise the faithful would have found it difficult to believe Christ was the ultimate minister of their sacraments. Goldenberg makes the further link, more dubious in my view, that without exclusively male ministers God could not continue to be the traditional (male) Christian deity.

There is good reason to doubt that the Christian God has to be conceived in male terms, and so good reason to question Goldenberg's assumption that feminism must mean the end of the Christian God. But one cannot blame non-Christian feminists from getting wrong ideas about Christian theology when popes botch central matters, and Goldenberg is certainly correct in judging that Christ and God the Father have made divinity male in most Christians' psyches. Moreover, she is on the mark in her conclusion about feminists' rejection of Paul VI's argument that women's exclusion from the priesthood does not render them inferior to men:

> Feminists understand that if women are not sufficiently "in the image of God" to be priests, then they are certainly considered inferior to men. No amount of prose extolling the harmony of keeping men and women in "separate but equal" roles can change the fact that men are reserving the most important roles for themselves. To gain true equality in Christianity women must have access to the positions that religion holds to be highest and best (p. 6).

So the core of the feminist challenge to the received notions of Christian selfhood is that the Church's practice has sullied its high claims almost irreparably; for in its practice, both distant and recent, the Church has sinned against women egregiously. While saying that in Christ there is neither male nor female (Gal. 3:28), the Church has discriminated against women systematically. While making love the crux of Christian morality, the Church has come close to hating women, penalizing them for their sex, in no way loving female nature as well as male. While preaching that perfect love is supposed to cast out fear (I John 4:18), the Church's treatment of women has been so imperfect, so fear-riddled, that frequently it has been far worse than that of secular society. Even today, many churches grant women fewer rights in ecclesiastical law than secular societies grant women in civil law.

So, the church has dug itself a great credibility gap. You cannot claim to be a light to the Gentiles, lag behind the Gentiles in sexual justice, and have your claim be found credible. You cannot lecture the world about human dignity, deny the full humanity of more than half your own membership, and have your lecturing be found credible. The Christian abuse of women therefore is a major scandal, a great millstone hung round its clerical neck. A truly religious Church would do penance and make reparation speedily, lest the Just Judge's patience give way to wrath.

This charge of male chauvinism runs through a full agenda of issues, undermining the Church's influence on such matters as abortion, contraception, homosexuality, and divorce. In the case of abortion, the Church's sinful sexism prevents many from hearing its wise concern for life, its valid fears about life's cheapening. In the case of contraception, the churches that still oppose "artificial" means tend to be so blighted by male bias that even their own members do not heed their teaching. This is manifestly true in Roman Catholicism, where about two-thirds of the married membership judges the official teaching on birth control unpersuasive. The "homophobia" of many Christian churches, their terror of gay people, runs in tandem with a general sexual unease (most of whose burdens women have borne), while divorced Christians have had their problems exacerbated in many communities because the Church's desire for stability and sexual control has outweighed its desire for compassion.

In all these matters the Protestant mainline churches have done better than the Catholic and Orthodox, but the performance of the Church overall has made it hard for feminists to place Christianity on the side of the angels. With more than sufficient evidence, feminists have concluded that Christianity makes people crazy in sexual matters, especially men. So, most feminists have labeled Christianity a foe of their sexual self and vowed to oppose it implacably.

3/Sociology

CHAPTER FIVE: CHRISTIAN SOCIAL THEORY

Our order in Parts I and II has placed feminist exposition first and Christian exposition second. In Parts III and IV we shall reverse this order, so as to foster equality in our two-way reflection. An admirable woman who has worked both sides of the feminist-Christian relation is Rosemary Ruether. Seeing Christianity as a foe of her feminine self, Ruether has vowed to oppose it implacably, so long as it remains mired in sexist sin. Because she is a fine theologian, however, she has been able to root this opposition in Christianity's own original soil, turning the cry of the biblical prophets for justice against the unjust Christian establishment. Through this work, Ruether's political style has become socialist. Let us therefore open our investigation of current Christian social theory with a recent study in which Ruether has tried to show the affinities between socialism and feminism.[1]

Insofar as "socialism" means Marxism, affinities have not

been patent. "Many in the feminist movement think that any connection of Marxism with feminism automatically means the subordination of the feminist agenda to male priorities in the name of 'the working class.' Marxists, in turn, have often regarded feminism with suspicion as a bourgeois movement" (p. 103). For Ruether, the alliance between Marxism and feminism can begin with the parallels between the two movements' critiques of religion. Marx saw religion as an ideology of the ruling class, a cultural superstructure and expresson of "alienation" (the objective situation in which one group is in the power of another). Engels and later Marxists added more positive judgments, largely because they found the teachings of the apocalyptic Christian sects very similar to their own.

Feminists, too, have criticized religion as an ideology; in their case, one that has supported male rule of a sexual caste system. As is true of Marxist studies of alienation, feminist studies of patriarchal bias have found the situation complicated. For example, the idealized woman, the Virgin Mother Mary, and the sinful woman, Eve, have tallied to a highly ambivalent imagery for women in Christian society. In addition, the idealized Christian view of women led, by many historical twists and turns, to the Victorian heritage with which we still contend today: "Home and work, female and male, have become complementary symbols in modern culture. Males are seen as secular, rational, egotistic, combative, sexual, oriented toward power and strenuous manipulation of the physical realities of the world. Women, by contrast, are religious, spiritual, asexual, virtuous, altruistic, irrational, dependent, and weak" (p. 105).

Out of this heritage comes the dilemma many current feminists face. On the one hand, women need to be the same as men: to have the same abilities, do the same jobs, et cetera. On the other hand, women need to be superior to men: in virtue, the nurturing qualities associated with motherhood, et cetera. Marxist feminism, under Engel's lead, placed the solution to women's oppression in their restoration to economic autonomy. Ruether finds this solution germane today, and she considers it a strong challenge to any elitist, "countercultural feminism." Integrating women into the high-status professions does little for the 97 percent of working women in sex-segregated, low-status, low-paying jobs.

Nonetheless, the socialist economics that derive from Marxist inspiration have enacted women's equalization only partially. As is true of liberal movements for women's equality, the unconscious model has remained the male work world. As a result, women continue to compete under a handicap, for they continue to be responsible for the domestic sphere even when they are laboring alongside men on the assembly line. To be true to its own stated goals of returning ownership of the means of production to the people, socialism would have to restore the pre-industrial conditions in which the home was society's main workshop.

From feminism, then, comes the plea for a two-way shift in sex roles, so that both male work and female domesticity can become spheres where equality reigns. Moreover, from feminism also comes one of the strongest pleas that work serve people, rather than vice-versa. Therefore, feminism can help restore to socialism the central questions of meaning that an alienated, dehumanized society has neglected.

GRASS-ROOTS COMMUNITIES I

Ruether's socialism is of a piece with the views of many Latin American liberation theologians, who are employing Marxist tools of class analysis to delineate the politico-economic changes their countries need. Without withdrawing my admiration for what such socialism seems to intend, I feel the need to note the sobering historical studies of Eric Voegelin and Igo Shafarevich,[2] which indicate the great amount of unrealism that has stalked the major socialist thinkers and movements. I also feel the need to underscore the fact that a truly Christian community sponsors the contemplative virtues as well as the economic, helping people to escape the tyrannies of history not only through political struggle, but also through deep prayer, liturgy, poetry, dance, and other non-profit ventures. For though "the tyrannies of history" certainly first call to mind the brutal political regimes of both the right and the left, which subordinate human beings to money and power, it also calls to mind the world-views in which one never escapes time and the secular realm—in which everything is oppressively horizontal. Lacking a vertical dimension to balance their revolutionary labors, many socialists lose their grip and turn to cruelty or despair.

All the more impressive, then, are the grass-roots communities that are the backbone of the Latin American Christian revolution. Put off by the collusion of the institutional church with the going culture of repression, thousands of Latin Americans have banded together in small local groups *(comunidades de base)* to raise a Christian revolutionary consciousness and mutual support. Perhaps the most famous of such grass-roots communities was the Solentiname church in Nicaragua led by Ernesto Cardenal. The community was destroyed by the Somoza regime in 1977, but prior to that, it had functioned as a contemplative group dedicated to the needs of the local *campesinos*. It had a chapel, where the people gathered each Sunday to discuss the scriptures and celebrate the eucharist; a clinic, an artists' center, and fish and farm cooperatives. The people of the Solentiname Archipelago drew great strength from the community, as did Christian socialists all over the world. For Solentiname managed to be both political and religious, both practical and idealistic. One has only to read the scripture discussions of the people, many of whom were poor and uneducated, to see what challenges to oppressive regimes like the Somoza dictatorship the simple words of Jesus mount.[3]

Grass-roots or basic Christian communities have started to impinge on North American consciousness,[4] suggesting that, before long, Christian women here may begin to think of their communities in similar terms. To be sure, our economic conditions are quite different, for we Northerners tend to be a large part of the Latin Americans' problem, reaching in with our capitalist tentacles.[5] On the other hand, North American women are the ones who suffer most from the injustices of the North American economic system, so many of the charges of the Latin American poor echo eloquently in the lives of women of the North. We tend not to suffer so dramatically for our opposition to the status quo, however, nor to suffer so faith-fully. The report of the Women for Dialogue *(Mujeres para el Dialogo)* seminar held in Mexico October 1 to October 5, 1979 makes this characterization quite concrete.[6]

The opening number of the Women's Seminar document sounds the theme that dominates the whole: "In October 1979 we, a group of women involved in people's movements, have met for the first time to reflect on the situation of oppression confronting women and their contribution to the revolutionary struggle. Our reflections are made in the light of faith, and our aim is to organize them theologically in ecumenical terms" (p. 25). The twenty-four participants, twenty women and four men, gathered near Tepeyac, the sacred hillside of Tontantzin, the mother-goddess who consoled the Aztecs, where present-day Mexicans venerate Our Lady of Guadalupe. They came from Brazil, Colombia, Costa Rica, Peru, Argentina, Cuba, the United States, and Mexico. At the conclusion of the Seminar they held an ecumenical service led by a woman from Cuba who was an ordained Presbyterian minister. The aside that the document makes at the end of its introductory section should ring ominously in Vatican corridors: "We also wish to point out that our seminar coincided with the visit of the pope to the United States, where he manifested the position of the ecclesiastical hierarchy against women. It symbolizes the historic struggle that we women have to wage within the church" (p. 25).

In detailing the various oppressions of the Latin American woman, the Seminar makes it clear that she is the lowest of the low, especially if she is Indian, *mestiza,* or black. Economically, politically, and culturally, she is marginal to the prevailing structures of power. Both at work and at home, she suffers the effects of Latin machismo, as well as the grinding poverty of an area where the gulf between rich and poor is enormous. However, the Seminar insists that this should not lead women to separate their cause from that of the general struggle. Only bourgeois women's movements, lacking class consciousness, would do that.

GRASS-ROOTS COMMUNITIES II

Like Ruether, then, the Seminar wants women to be sensitive to class as well as sexual discriminations. That is not to say the Seminar minces words about sexual discrimination, especially in the Latin American Church. On the contrary, it states clearly that the church is a patriarchal structure supporting the status quo. The Church excludes women from most decision-making, and often is itself a model of an oppressive man-woman relationship. Nonetheless, despite the opposition they face as women, these Christian revolutionaries pledge their full strength to the popular movement for justice. Simply put, this is the struggle of Latin America's poor for equity. The link between such a struggle for equity and an evangelical faith should be obvious, but it is only in the small grass-roots communities, which resemble both the early churches of the catacombs and Communist cells, that such obvious links have begun to be made.

For example, throughout the discussions of the Solentiname community one can almost feel the group's consciousness rise to grasp new connections among the different forms of oppression. Consider the following extract from a discussion of John 8:1-11, the text on the woman taken in adultery:

> TERESITA: "I believe all the men who were accusing that woman were adulterers." OSCAR: "It seems there were great

oppressions at that time, right? And one of them was that a woman was treated like dirt, because if she, the female, did it, it was terrible; if the man did it they didn't even notice." OLIVA: "It was the *machismo* of that time, which was very strong, but we go right on having it in our time. That woman didn't commit adultery all by herself, and the man she committed adultery with, they didn't accuse him." OSCAR: "Yes, they didn't bring him." . . . ROGER PEREZ, the young painter from Managua: "The case of this woman is important for us in Latin America. We need to learn this lesson of tolerance and pardon and love in the case of the adultery of the woman. We've had a tradition opposed to this for centuries, the *machismo* tradition. Among us the adulterous woman is still condemned to death, and not just in songs. There are phrases that we all repeat: "If she did a thing like that to me, I'd kill her, that bitch." This isn't Christian, it isn't revolutionary."[7]

Class consciousness and consciousness of sexism therefore merge in the grass-roots communities that have strong women. They would seem to offer North American Christian feminists a wonderful model. Focusing on the scriptures and the eucharist, their meetings insist that the gospel become a message of liberation right here and now. Unless it is good news to the local poor, it has been eviscerated. The grass-roots groups also seem to draw from their particularity a strong impulse to place themselves in the tradition of the entire Church.[8] They seem to realize that the word they ponder, the flesh they consume, has nourished millions through the centuries, and that it enlivens many other downtrodden people in other parts of the globe today. Indeed, wherever brothers and sisters are struggling for justice in faith, the grass-roots community has a sibling church. So, for example, the struggles of African Christians for liberation should be very encouraging to the Latin Americans.[9]

Of course, the move from a small church, pivoted on Word and Sacrament, to a full feminist social theory is considerable, but certain Christian convictions could help feminists toward a global vision of the community they seek.

Christianity says, for instance, that the future community should be inclusive, not exclusive. It should make room for both sexes, all races, all social classes, and all human needs. The poor and marginal have a special claim on this future community, because they have been especially abused in the past. Women deserve a special hearing, for they have been under-heard in the past (and that under-hearing has contributed mightily to our present systems of injustice).

A grass-roots community, like a coven, is small enough to allow all its members to participate. It is small enough for members to get to know one another, care for one another, realize when someone is hurt or missing. In the *comunidad de base* there is greater inclination toward music, dance, and poetry than there is in larger social groups. There is greater inclination to see life in the round, and so to think of cooperatives for child-care, selling people's products, securing medical services, and the like. One could imagine a worse social order than a series of federations of grass-roots communities. The model may not completely fit the highly developed technological societies (although note one feminist notion of urban planning in the next chapter), but it does fit most of the situations of the world's majority, who are poor, disspirited, and almost mortally in need of cooperatives. Were a model like this to be developed by feminist theologians, we could even see a renewed Mariology, summarized in the prophetic witness of the Magnificat: "He has put down the mighty from their thrones, and exalted those of low degree" (Luke 1:52).

LITURGY

We shall come momentarily to some feminist challenges to a Christian social vision like that implied in the *comunidades de base,* but before hearing these feminist caveats let us attend to liturgy, the "work of the people" at the center of the Christian social vision. Since there are now women priests from the catholic (episcopal) tradition, our reflections can step off from some comments of a feminist eucharistic celebrant, Patricia Park. She is describing the first public eucharistic celebration of the eleven episcopal women ordained "irregularly" in 1974:

> I was familiar with women in the ministry of the Word. I yearned to see another woman bless and feed us with the body and blood of our Lord Jesus Christ. Finally the time came. Because I was the assistant deacon, I stood to Carter Heyward's right. She raised up her arms and sang, "The Lord be with you." The response came back, "And also with you." "Lift up your hearts." "We lift them up unto the Lord." I was transfixed on that spot. The church seemed to radiate, people spoke and hugged and cried with each other.[10]

Park goes on to describe the fittingness of women's mediating the eucharist and the other Christian sacraments. From her own pastoral experience, she makes the case eloquently that the Church is impoverished when its priesthood excludes women. It is the special significance of the eucharist for Christian social theory that I want to develop, however, for the eucharist is the sign *par excellence* of the Church assembled as the avant garde of a new, liberated humanity.

The eucharist dramatizes the Christian story of salvation. Its word and action are an anamnesis, a remembering into the present of God's past interventions on human beings' behalf. As the Eastern Christians have emphasized, God intervened to save mortal humanity from death. The eucharist is therefore a "medicine" for immortality. As the Western Christians have emphasized, God intervened to save mortal humanity from sin. The eucharist is therefore a sacrament of reconciliation, at least as much as penance is. And God's salvation from both mortality and sin is a work of love, a recreation in love. The eucharist is therefore above all a love-feast, an *agape*. When they gather at the eucharist, Christians ought to remember these formative convictions and emotions into the present. Were they to do so, making the Christian liturgy effective, the Christian world-view would quickly take flame.

In the spectrum of world-views, the Christian one stands out for the audacity of its hope. Because of a specific man, who, it believes, passed over to God's heaven, Christianity usually leans forward into the future expecting forgiveness and immortality. That is why Park's unabashed confession of faith in Christ's body and blood struck me so forcibly. It has the ring of the genuine tradition, however much it is liable to magical abuse. The bread and wine that Christians consume are food for a life that goes far beyond what secular prudence allows. It is a life entailing precisely the things that can free small communities and make them havens of liberation. What things? An open future, where new beginnings are possible. The forgiveness of old sins and debts. The burning of old vices and debilities in a more consuming passion. The imitation of Christ, who gave himself for others. There is no Christian vision without these things, and they should come alive in each eucharist.

Applied specifically to such social dysfunctions as economic injustice, sexism, and racism, the eucharistic liturgy ought to cut two ways. Challengingly, it ought to measure the gap between gospel standards and the prevailing social mores. For example, preachers should all but categorically denounce a wage system that condemns the black and female working populations to semi-human status. It should read out of the Church any preference for profits over people. Much that goes on in the munitions, tobacco, and chemical industries simply can't be done by a Christian in objectively good conscience. Church officials have a right to caution against moralistic harshness, a right to urge prudence, but their own timidity halves that right. By not naming the enemies of Christian humaneness forthrightly, they have contributed strongly to our culture's war, disease, and ecological devastation.

Yet, consolingly, the eucharistic liturgy always holds out a chance of new beginnings. If sinners repent, God promises them forgiveness, even seventy times seven. Indeed, God requires their brothers and sisters to forgive them seventy times seven. This dynamic of challenge and forgiveness has a power I have seen nowhere else, a power I long to see feminism embrace.

FEMINIST REFLECTIONS I

There are secular analogues to this dynamic of challenge and forgiveness, and while, in my opinion, they do not have the depth of the Christian eucharist, they often have an exactness or passion that puts sleepytown Christianity to shame. For example, Adrienne Rich's essay "Disloyal to Civilization: Feminism, Racism, Gynephobia"[11] discusses the relations between feminism and racism with a candor that few Christian discussions can match. If we follow her passionate exposition, and then set it in the lines of a eucharistic challenge-and-forgiveness, we may glimpse the sacramental Christian feminism that priests such as Park one day could lead.

The topic of feminist-black relations obviously had troubled Rich for some time before the writing of her essay, and she saw it as a minefield:

> It is difficult to begin writing the words that will carry my own thoughts on feminism and racism beyond the confines of my own mind, this room. It is difficult because I wish to be understood, because I write at a crossroads which is mined with pain and anger, and because I do not want my words to lend themselves to distortion or expropriation, either by apologists for a shallow and trivial notion of feminism, or by exponents of a racial politics that denies the fundamental nature of sexual politics and gender oppression (p. 279).

Rich's own lesbian feminism sought a profound transformation of the hitherto prevailing social relationships, such that both race and sex would assume a new configuration, born of women's new consciousness and solidarity against male oppression.

Much of the essay then turns to historical topics, documenting from the emerging literature on American racial and sexual history the bonds of false consciousness that have tied white women, especially in the South but also in the North, to enslaved blacks. Many white women who were repelled by slavery drew back from the radical implications of their feelings, for had they followed these feelings they would have confronted a sexual slavery all too similar. With the rise of black consciousness in the twentieth century, certain bonds that had been forged by the abolitionists, many of whom saw the need to enfranchise both blacks and women, split apart.

The result was considerable bad blood between blacks and feminists, a result that Rich lays at men's door:

> The charge of "racism" flung at white women in the earliest groups of the independent feminist movement was a charge made in the most obscene bad faith by white "radical" males (and by some Leftist women) against the daring leap of self-definition needed to create an autonomous feminist analysis. That leap, as group after group, woman after woman, has discovered, often involves feelings of extreme dislocation, "craziness," and terror. For many white feminists, the cynical and manipulative use of the charge of "racism" as a deterrent to feminist organizing was one bitter source of disenchantment with the male-dominated Left (along with the visible male supremacism both of the Left and of men in the black movement). It corresponded, for us, to the charge black feminists have had to withstand, of "fragmenting" the black struggle or "castrating" the black man. In other words, and ironically, the more deeply a woman might recognize and hate the fact of racist oppression (and many of the first white independent feminists had learned its realities in the civil rights movement in the South), the more vulnerable she felt in her struggle to define a politics which would, for once, take the position of women as central, and which would perceive the oppression of women both as a political reality embedded in

every institution, and as a permeating metaphor throwing light on every other form of domination (p. 290).

Rich continues in this line, writing white-hot prose fresh from the vats of pain. Whatever self-indulgence her tactic entails is more than outweighed by the depth of insight it achieves. When Rich finally comes to the reconciliations of black and white women, she has portrayed their mutual suffering so vividly that one can almost feel the healing in their embrace. It is nothing merely notional or cerebral. Heart to heart, womb to womb, the two groups of women whose histories have been so tangled can struggle for a new sisterhood. The dynamic of challenge and forgiveness has moved the essay and, one hopes, the history of black and white women, forward toward a genuinely new humanity. Surely a generous Christian theology of grace can see this new humanity as a prominent part of the Pauline new creation.

I am well aware that Adrienne Rich probably cares very little about Pauline or Johannine new creations. For her, Christianity probably is a bastion of male supremacy, and so a bastion of the enemy. Indeed, if Rich can accuse Robert Coles of vampirizing the lives of the oppressed (p. 302), few outside her radical lesbian camp are likely to be safe. Nonetheless, I run the risk of being called a shallow feminist or an expropriator of other's passion because I want the truth in Rich's essay to engage the Christian social vision. We Christians must get far beneath the namby-pamby level at which we now deal with most of our social problems, if we are to experience genuine healing in the blood of Christ. Whether it be questions of sex, race, or economic injustice, people who have been racked and torn by our social evils are not going to be made whole by a dab of holy water. No cheap grace of easy repentance, of formulaic breast-beating followed by business as usual, is going to change things so that they become worthy of Christian freedom. The manifest superiority of Christianity as a world-view, its concern for the beginning and end of things that radical feminism blithely ignores, regularly is vitiated by Christianity's manifest inferiority on the level of emotional honesty. All too often, the churches are refuges from social conscience, tallowed halls where seldom is heard an accusatory word and justice is not demanded all day.

FEMINIST REFLECTIONS II

Adrienne Rich attributes much of our present Western injustice to gynephobia: fear of women. One senses she considers this a culpable fear, little different from Mary Daly's "hatred of the feminine." And, like Daly, Rich spins out a system practically unfalsifiable, placing the full burden of our present injustices and misperceptions on men, so as to leave separatist feminists in the clear. Reviewing Daly's *Gyn/Ecology,* Ross Kraemer has likened this system to an ancient Gnosticism.[12] I find this an interesting characterization, for it props the charge of "unrealism" I have advanced at several points. However, the characterization also calls to mind the several virtues of Gnostic Christianity, high among which was a greater respect for the feminine, in both divinity and society, than became the rule in orthodox Christianity. Elaine Pagels has argued that orthodox Christianity stamped out the Gnostic variety largely for political reasons,[13] and this seems a good place to consider the feminist implications of her charge.

In dealing with the Gnostic texts discovered at Nag Hammadi in Upper Egypt, Pagels observes that there is:

> one striking difference between these "heretical" sources and orthodox ones: gnostic sources continually use sexual symbolism to describe God. One might expect that these texts would show the influence of archaic traditions of the Mother Goddess, but for the most part, their language is specifically Christian, unmistakably related to a Jewish heritage. Yet instead of describing a monistic and masculine God, many of these texts speak of God as a dyad who embraces both masculine and feminine elements (p. 49).

Concerning the feminine elements, the Gnostics described God in terms of an eternal, mystical silence. They also spoke of Her as the Holy Spirit and Wisdom. In the Gnostic poem called the *Thunder, Perfect Mind,* the feminine power speaks most provocatively:

> I am the first and the last.
> I am the honored one and the scorned one.
> I am the whore, and the holy one.
> I am the wife and the virgin.
> I am (the mother) and the daughter. . . .
> I am she whose wedding is great, and I have not taken a husband. . . .
> I am knowledge, and I am fear. . . .
> I am foolish, and I am wise. . . .
> I am godless, and I am one whose God is great (pp. 55-56).

It is true enough that one can draw from texts such as this an underlying intuition of androgyny. In both divinity and humanity, the female as well as the male analogues beg full consideration. Yet one can also see such a text as simply mental meandering. Having wandered onto a path of facile contrast, the author just potters along, juxtaposing one thought with another. So, where the Gnostics accused the Christians of having a jealous God, whose fear of the original Mother led Him to demand the removal of all her feminine traces, mental weakness may play a greater role, the Gnostic dyad of male and female becoming a garbled bit of jabberwocky.

On the other hand, the parallel between the Gnostic political and theological structures lends credence to Pagels' suspicion that the Christians rejected the feminist Gnostic theology for practical as well as philosophical reasons. Among such Gnostic groups as the Valentinians, for example, the female divinity supported women's equality to men. Many women in such groups were prophets, teachers, traveling evangelists, healers, priests, and perhaps even bishops. This "heretical" tendency may have loomed all the larger because of egalitarian trends in the larger culture. In Greece and Asia Minor, women were participating with men in the cults of the Great Mother and the Egyptian Goddess Isis. In Roman society man and woman increasingly were binding themselves with new, voluntary, and mutual vows. As well, Roman women were involving themselves in business, social life, sporting events, and traveling. Jewish women, on the contrary, were excluded from active participation in public worship, education, and social and political life. Despite an early history in which their women were very active, by the year 200, the majority of the Christian communities had chosen the Jewish model, endorsing such restrictive views as that of I Timothy 2:11-12: "Let a woman learn in silence in all submissiveness. I permit no woman to teach or to have authority over men; she is to keep silent."

Pagels shows that neither the orthodox Christian nor the Gnostic side of this struggle was monolithic. A Clement of Alexandria felt free to use female imagery for God, while many of the Gnostics so feared sexuality that they wrote bitter texts against female nature. In the Christian case, though, a male theology and polity prevailed. As God was superior to the human being, so the male was superior to the female. The traditions of the biblical past, where masculinity prevailed in both theology and social life, made enough sense in the Hellenistic world to convince the Christians that patriarchy would serve the Church well. We have few records of women's judgments in this matter, but we know that no feminist separatist movement won the day, any more than a strict egalitarian movement did.

The lesson I see in this bit of history is the intertwining of the four realms of reality with which we constantly deal. Theology, psychology, sociology, and ecology so interrelate that certain logical "runs" are almost bound to carry across several realms. Just as the orthodox Christians were pressured to fit their theology to their politics, so today's radical feminists are pressured to fit their thealogy to their politics. But a further lesson from the Gnostic episode is the danger of withdrawing from reality as a whole. The Gnostics withdrew when they could not face sexuality or Jesus' history. The radical lesbians withdraw when they cannot stand men. But reality as a whole—the earth under one's feet, the neighbor of a different sex next door, the customs of the barbarians across the river, and the Mystery of beginning and beyond—argues that we must stay in touch, must build our "world" from sensible contact as well as creative imagination. When we heed this argument, reality as a whole offers us the consolation that few images are absolute, few customs are ironclad. Only honesty and love have sovereign rights, in sociology as well as theology. Only dishonest and unloving lifestyles are *verboten,* and the Goddess alone finally decides which they are.

CHAPTER SIX: FEMINIST POLITICAL THEORY

As "theology" and "psychology" have proven to be broad terms, admitting items from religious ritual or literature, so "sociology" is a broad term, having to cover the entire realm of social relations. I use "political theory" in a similar spirit, making it bear the weight of various feminist reflections on how the *polis,* the human commonweal, might better prosper. To begin with a theme from the previous chapter, we can note a significant feminist agreement that grass-roots communities could be crucial to the future of human social intercourse. Dolores Hayden's interesting study, "What Would a Non-Sexist City Be Like? Speculations on Housing, Urban Design, and Human Work,"[1] launches this theme quite practically.

Hayden begins by observing that the dictum, "A woman's place is in the home," has been a very important (if usually implicit) assumption of the male-dominated design professions. However, as women have come to enter the paid labor force in huge numbers, this implicit assumption has proven inaccurate, bringing much of our urban design into crisis.

> Dwellings, neighborhoods, and cities designed for homebound women constrain them physically, socially, and economically. Acute frustration occurs when women defy these constraints to spend all or part of the work day in the paid labor force. I contend that the only remedy for this situation is to develop a new paradigm of the home, the neighborhood, and the city; to begin to describe the physical, social, and economic design of a human

settlement that would support, rather than restrict, the activities of employed women and their families (p. S171).

Such a human settlement, in support of working women, would have to reverse the suburban sprawl of single-family homes grouped in class-segregated areas, with their freeways, shopping centers, and commercial strip developments. To summon just one epitomizing statistic, the prevailing pattern has brought us to the point where the United States (6 percent of the world's population) uses 41 percent of the world's passenger cars. We all know the dream the pattern whispered: (male) workers would return from the office or factory, located in the ugly city, to a serene, suburban environment maintained by their (female) spouses.

When women began to revolt from their side of this dream, challenging the feminine mystique, the suburban planners' vision became a nightmare. It assumed private cooking, cleaning, child care, and transportation of adults and children. It removed the family from any shared community space: day-care facilities, schools, etc. It assumed full-time care for the house, and it showed its horrible isolation in such stress situations as wife-battering: every thirty seconds a woman is being battered somewhere in the United States, usually in the kitchen or bedroom of her own home. More often than not, she cannot escape. Her isolated house has become her torture chamber.

As women who become the support of a household quickly learn, society badly serves those who must both work and care for a home. Only when we overcome the traditional divisions between the marketplace and the household will some measure of efficiency visit single working mothers' situations. Hayden uses a major portion of her space to report on projects in other countries that offer more efficient, helpful housing facilities, as a first step toward a non-sexist urban environment.

The "service houses" of Sweden, for example, provide child care and cooked food, along with housing for employed women and their families. The Steilshoop Project of Hamburg, Germany, is even more ambitious, including a number of former mental patients as residents, in addition to providing support services for the public-housing tenants. The Fiona House project in London is designed to facilitate shared baby-sitting, and it opens its day-care center to neighborhood residents for a fee. This offers the single parents jobs as day-care workers, and helps the neighborhood's working parents. This arrangement suggests that home and work need not be separated or opposed.

The United States has its own tradition of utopian socialist experiments, including the commune movement of the 1960s, and Hayden draws on this tradition to sketch the basic principles for what she calls HOMES (Homemakers Organization for a More Egalitarian Society). These principles include: 1) involving men and women equally in unpaid housework and child care; 2) involving men and women equally in the paid work force; 3) eliminating residential segregation by class, race, and age; 4) eliminating governmental programs and laws that reenforce the unpaid role of the female homemaker; 5) minimizing unpaid domestic labor and wasteful energy consumption; 6) maximizing households' choices regarding recreation and socializing. Fully sketched, down to model neighborhood plans, Hayden's HOMES shows that the feminist reconstruction of social space is well under way.

I find it useful to step back from such blueprints and ruminate on the attitudinal changes an egalitarian, non-sexist social design would require. What strikes me most forcibly is that it would demand we become members of one another. Neither women's needs, nor the needs of other outcaste groups, such as the aged or the racially marginal, will be met so long as our individualistic model of political instruction continues to obtain. The invisible hand that was supposed to direct our individualistic strivings to the greatest good for the greatest number is palpably spastic nowadays, as the poor have always found it to be. For truly significant social change, something approaching a religious conversion seems necessary.

ANTHROPOLOGICAL PERSPECTIVES

The egalitarian society envisioned by projections such as HOMES sometimes runs into the anthropological objection that male dominance is the rule in all the societies of which we are aware. This objection is in part based on research stemming from a reaction to the nineteenth-century views of Bachofen and Morgan, who argued that society early in human history had had a matriarchal structure. As feminist sensitivities have begun to infiltrate anthropology, however, scholars have begun to qualify the thesis of the universality of male dominance.

> There is a certain bias to this point of view, a bias that is understandable given the Western equation of dominance with public leadership. By defining dominance differently, one can show that in many societies male leadership is balanced by female authority. For example, among the Ashanti, Iroquois, and Dahomeans, although women were not as visible as men in external public affairs, their right to veto male actions suggests a bipartite system of checks and balances in which neither sex dominated the other.[2]

In other words, without the Western bias in favor of male dominance, women's influence in other societies emerges as considerably stronger, making an egalitarian future much less utopian.

To be sure, studies of how societies actually operate almost always have found that women hold considerable informal power and influence.[3] Feminist anthropologists seem to be discovering, however, that many societies legitimate this power and influence more formally than we do in the technological West. Indeed, in some tribal societies the women so delegate "focal leadership" to the men that the women clearly are the *source* of the men's social power. In many such cases, the women even retain a veto over the male focal leaders' actions. But why should women choose this roundabout way of running things? When they have power, why do they not run things themselves?

> The answer lies in the proposition . . . that it is more efficient for women to delegate than to monopolize power. Since women are the potential bearers of new additions to the population, it would scarcely be expedient to place them on the front line at the hunt and in warfare. In addition, there are such questions as: What would there be for men to do if women hunted, warred, or ruled? How would men acquire the "reason for being" that comes to women automatically?[4]

It is this "automatic," fertility power of women that underlies the dual-sex political systems of West Africa. In such systems, each sex has its own autonomous sphere of authority, as well as an area of shared responsibility. Other cultural areas actually give women a preponderance of social power. For example, in the matrifocal societies of Southeast Asia, women generally are the producers and control the economic resources. Kinswomen stay in frequent contact through mutual aid groups, and women tend to make at least as many decisions, to be at least as assertive, as men. The role of the mother is ritually significant, and women on the whole can support and care for their children with little help from men.

Their economic significance plays a similarly important role in the equality of many women of small-scale tribes. In foraging societies, for example, women tend to achieve power in the measure that the group's survival depends on their gathering. This is the case, for instance, with the !Kung women of the Kalahari Desert in Africa. Although these women do not hunt, they serve the male hunters as scouts, bringing back reports on "the state of the bush." Hunting is the most prestigious activity, because meat is the preferred food, but since !Kung women gather 60 percent to 80 percent of the daily food intake by weight, they have a solid social equality. "!Kung females are autonomous and participate in group decisions because they do not need the assistance of men at any stage in the production of gathered food. Nor do they need the permission of men to use any natural resources entering into this production."[5]

The roles of men and women in other societies show a similar equalization, when anthropologists study them without the prejudice of Western notions of power. Thus Ojibwa women have been found who learn hunting skills from male relatives and become successful hunters and trappers. Menomini culture allowed for "deviant" women, who preferred male roles such as judge, council member, and the like. Women traders predominate in West Africa, the non-Hispanic Caribbean, and some parts of mainland Latin America. Vietnamese consider women more economical, thrifty, and suited for the demanding work of trade. Phillipine men leave small-scale market trade to their wives, and large-scale trade to foreigners, because the coarse language and aggressive behavior that trade involves ill fit the Phillipine male image.

In many cases, therefore, women's economic power goes hand in hand with a sexual division of labor. Women then come to control an independent sphere of cultural activity, and so to achieve self-sufficiency. When such a sphere has the added support of a magico-religious power, usually based on female fertility, women's status is quite secure. When the religious or traditional legal supports are weak, rapid change, such as that introduced by Westernization, can quickly strip women of their status and power. So, for example, women have been losing their traditional predominance in African trade, as Western influence has opened new opportunities for men.

Overall, women remain more powerful in plant than in animal economies. When technological change overtakes a plant economy, women tend to lose their access to strategic resources, and so their traditional measures of power. Still, if the creation myths of the society extoll feminine power, women's status tends to remain high. It is the *cultural* invasions of colonialism, destroying the mythic basis of the traditional society, that have most displaced tribal women.

FAMILY-CENTERED POLITICS

When anthropologists and other social scientists look at women's political roles cross-culturally, they tend to focus on idiosyncratic emotional outbursts. Where men play the prominent power games, and act in fairly predictable patterns, women manipulate feelings within the family. Recently feminist consciousness has occasioned a second look at these feminine outbursts and manipulations. If Jane Fishburne Collier's essay "Women in Politics"[6] is accurate, women's actions are far more predictable, and far more intrinsic to a given group's political alignments, than social scientists hitherto have realized.

This remains likely despite the perhaps debatable and distasteful model that Collier's argument assumes:

> The model woman of my argument . . . is not the affectionate daughter, hard-working wife, or loving mother who gets into trouble while trying to make the best of a difficult situation, but the cold, calculating female who uses all available resources to control the world around her. My model woman seeks power: the capacity to determine her own and others' actions (p. 90).

Natives themselves resist viewing women in this light, because the domestic context of women's power-struggles means that the fierce competitors are close kin. It is more palatable for their cruel words and nasty deeds to appear as spontaneous outbursts than as abuse coldly calculated for political ends.

Although women are almost always at some disadvantage in competing for political power and prestige, cross-culturally their handicap is least when 1) leadership rests on ability and 2) there is little separation between the domestic and public spheres. In political systems where the main decisions are made outside the home, women tend to be defined as legal minors. For example, societies with patrilocal extended households tend to give overt prestige and authority only to men. A woman who seeks power in such a situation therefore must do it through a male, usually her son: "by the time a man marries, he is already tied to his mother and has been taught to put the interests of his natal family before those of his stranger-bride" (p. 92).

A recurring theme of the literature on societies with patrilocal extended households is the belief that women at large are irresponsible and sexually threatening, while mothers are warm and self-sacrificing. This indicates how well power-seeking mothers have done their job. Collier thinks that Christian tradition offers an instance of this theme in its types of Eve and Mary. Where wives or sexually available women resemble Eve, trying to tempt men away from God and right, mothers resemble Mary, devoting themselves to their sons.

Of course, the same woman who would be Mary to her son must be Eve to her husband, but the ambiguity of the model for the individual woman need not lessen its political acuteness. Indeed, patrilocal societies (such as traditional China and India) instinctively conceived the female life cycle as necessitating such ambiguity. In the years of early marriage, the young bride, a stranger to her new household, inevitably felt lonely and unhappy. When she gave birth to children, especially sons, she entered on a period of usefulness and competence. In old age she could expect to wield considerable power, even to grow domineering. The main political point is that the astute young mother would realize that her fortunes lay with her sons and so would strive mightily to increase their prospects.

Specifically, the ambitious woman would use her wiles to increase her sons' inheritance and persuade her husband to set up a separate household, apart from that of his parents. This would place her in direct opposition to her mother-in-law, who had labored for decades to establish the family's extended household. The son clearly would be caught in the middle, the center of the two women's tempestuous ragings.

In male company, he would add his bit to the store of wisdom on women's selfish and quarrelsome nature, reenforcing the male group's tendency to treat women as legal minors—and to ignore the political significance of what was occurring.

For social groups such as the Zinacantan Mayas of Chiapas, Mexico, whom Collier herself studied, the significance could be great indeed. These people spent great amounts of time and energy on domestic quarrels. Indeed, calming angry women was their major work of reconciliation. Further, the high divorce rate in Zinacantan caused lineages to be shallow, and so political followings grew up around wealthy individuals, rather than around relatives.

There appear to be analogues of this in other tribal societies, such as that of the Ndembu of Africa. Ndembu leaders try to attract their sisters and prevent their wives from leaving. The divorce rate is high, villages grow and dissolve, and the entire political gestalt is quite fluid. In all likelihood, women's familial upsets, their pressures on men to change, are a driving force behind the Ndembu shifts of political liaison and power. Obviously enough, a supposedly emancipated society such as that of the United States operates through different dynamics, but movement toward situations where (1) leadership rests on ability and (2) there is little separation between the domestic and public sphere would seem to be precisely what a feminist politics should encourage.

AN INTERNATIONAL FUTURE

While anthropologists illumine the family-centered politics of women in many traditional or small-scale societies, and American feminists and theologians ponder the political currents of contemporary Western society, a few persons of still broader vision study the international future. One such person is Elise Boulding, whose *Women in the Twentieth Century World*[7] concludes its international survey of women's current situation with a chapter entitled, "The Coming of the Gentle Society."

The chapter begins with the new consciousness focused by the World Conference of International Women's Year held in Mexico City in June, 1975. The Conference showed the new realization of women's sufferings and untapped potential for worldwide political contributions that more than a century of sustained feminist work had produced. Boulding is quick to delineate the major obstacle that stands in the way of worldwide action upon this realization:

> Many responsible officials see attention to "women's problems" as a distraction from the serious business of attending to the world crises of war, hunger, and resource depletion. Thus we have a paradox: at the very moment in history when the conceptual framework and the appropriate data base have been joined for an approach to the problems of war, hunger, and resource depletion involving the integration of the excluded half of the world's population into the problem-solving process, the tremendous anxieties engendered by the gravity of these crises render most decision makers unable to open their minds to the new perspective offered (p. 223).

The grossest face of the problem is the arms race, which Boulding calls the "ultimate pathology of the twentieth century." To do an effective plastic surgery on this face, however, we need new images that offer creative alternatives to the centralized planning that runs us into the current batch of cul-de-sacs. These new images would be of futures calling forth a decentralist yet interconnected and interdependent world. In turn, such images depend on a "deeply spiritual faith that humankind is something more, and human society meant to become something other than what we have realized so far in the human experience" (p. 227). And who is likely to produce such images? People marginal to the present society, excluded from the centers of power, who see society with a fresh eye. Then people whose marginal status had not excluded them from obtaining practical everyday skills, and who could help develop the intermediate social technology needed to replace the inefficient centralist methods, could go to work implementing thc images.

The largest such marginal group, of course, is the world's women. Excluded from the going corridors of power, they do not "belong" to the present systems as men do. Utilizing the metaphor of the family, where they have on the whole domiciled, such women might stress the dimensions of mutuality and sharing that a successful family situation must have. In this stress they would be countering the predominate male sense of the family, in which a strong father directs the lives of helpless children, but every likelihood is that women could more than hold their own on the family battleground.

The happy result for which Boulding hopes is a future society that is more androgynous or gentle. So long as militant feminists' argument that women's liberation means liberation from nurturant roles does not win the day, there seems a good chance that women's millennial sophistication in indirect, defusive ways of proceeding, through building networks and cooperating, could soon come into its own. The breakdown of central planning, the waste and poor quality it is creating throughout the advanced societies, argues that a better way will soon be able to get a fair hearing. No doubt, en route to that better way, some women will have to become more aggressive, and some men will have to become more nurturing. Overall, though, the joint direction we need is clear: toward an economics and politics whose approach to war, hunger, and resource depletion is gentler, more compassionate, more flexible and ad hoc.

Boulding suggests several leverage points where the application of pressure might speed up such social change. The first is the family, where the redefinition of gender-based roles is well under way, at least in Euro-American culture. When the ratio of women's opportunities for work reaches parity with men's, and men's responsibilities for child and home care reach a parity with women's, the smallest unit of society should be considerably more gentle. The second leverage point is the early-childhood school setting, where women now can exert a tremendous influence.

> By giving major attention to the further development of apprenticeship relationships between children and other sectors of the community, crossing not only age but economic, ethnic, and cultural boundaries, teachers can see to it that no set of skills becomes the exclusive domain of any one section of the community. By involving male volunteers more heavily in the educational experiences of children, teachers can promote the resocialization of both children and adults away from gender-based roles to social roles that express individual human capacities (pp. 235-36).

The community itself is a third leverage point; for example, through local initiative in reconstructing neighborhood self-help networks to deal with illness, child care, basic farming, food, and shelter. Women are the ones most likely to know where the hidden resources of the community are, and the ones most likely to be able to help boys and girls get the training they will need to share community tasks more equally. A fourth leverage point comes from the international declarations and covenants on human rights. When we apply their standards locally, so that our own country or state has to take its women's talents more seriously, the gentle society knocks at the door.

CHRISTIAN REFLECTIONS I

Elise Boulding clearly has a vision of the full future that the feminist revolution implies. In addition to a bevy of historical and economic facts, she has an intuition of how "gentleness" might balm the many places where the international order now suffers painful abrasion. As a result, her "idealism" is much more than a poetic projection. It stems from a hard look at humanity's current dysfunctions, joined to a faithful listening to her own spirit of faith, hope, and love.

It is the lack of such a full vision, spanning from practical facts to what Robert Coles' maid called "the end of things," that vitiates most of the feminist political science or philosophy one encounters. Accepting the terms of the male secular schools, most feminist theoreticians fail to step back and question those terms' adequacy. This is the case, for example, with Alison Jaggar's survey of political philosophies of women's liberation.[8] Though she deals clearly enough with the conservative, liberal, Marxist, and radical feminist camps, she never questions all four camps' neglect of the basic philosophical questions of beginning and beyond, of why there is something rather than nothing.

The conservative position, against which feminists are in reaction, says that differential treatment of women, as a group, is not unjust. Feminists limit the effectiveness of their attacks on such conservatism by failing to consider the end of human time, the final cause for which women and men manifestly labor equally. "The liberal feminist interprets equality to mean that each individual, regardless of sex, should have an equal opportunity to seek whatever social position she or he wishes. Freedom is primarily the absence of legal constraints to hinder women in this enterprise" (p. 259). This is basically the individualistic, competitive view that we have already criticized on several occasions. It runs in the lines of John Locke and Adam Smith, and all the marginalized peoples of modern Western history say that it makes bad economics and politics.

The Marxist feminists begin with the doctrinaire view that women's oppression, like all social evils, stems from the institution of private property. As a further wrinkle, they argue that monogamous marriage was designed to perpetuate the consolidation of wealth in the hands of a few (male) persons. Thus marriage is a sort of domestic slavery, and women's emancipation must go hand in hand with the abolition of the capitalist system. In the present era, before the state's ultimate demise, we should move toward the public assumption of the means of production. This philosophy presupposes "a very different account of human nature from that held by the liberal. Instead of seeing the individual as fundamentally concerned with the maximization of her or his own self-interest, the classical Marxist feminist believes that the selfish and competitive aspects of our natures are the result of their systematic perversion in an acquisitive society" (p. 261). As the various Marxist regimes, from the Soviet Union to Vietnam, suggest, this is a utopian view of human nature, in the pejorative sense. If the liberal view clearly has proven impotent to control the evils of individualistic selfishness, the Marxist view clearly has proven impotent to control the repressions of the state.

Radical feminism, in Jaggar's lexicon, takes its rise from the concept of sexual oppression. In its view, the most basic form of oppression, historically, was the physical subjugation of women by men. Thus the power-relationships that develop within the family are the most basic forms of oppression, in terms of which racial and economic injustices may best be understood. Many radical feminists look to new technologies to snap the link between sex and reproduction, and some go to the extreme of calling for the abolition of all gender-based differentiations.

It is striking to me that none of these feminist philosophies deals at all adequately with the basic *human* problems of death, malice, origin, and destiny. Thus the orientation in reality that the human person most needs for sanity goes by the boards. Where traditional societies formed their people for realistic living through cosmogonic and eschatological myths, the new philosophies go mute. By and large, they seem to assume that economics and politics are the sum of human existence. The price they would have us pay for sexual equality is the abdication of the human spirit's deepest need, which is for a comprehensive system of meaning. Nietzsche's dictum that "one who has a why can put up with any how" is liable to all sorts of abuse, but its core rings solid and true. The feminist views that Jaggar surveys, like most other contemporary philosophies, ignore this solid core. They are so uncontemplative, so ignorant of the millennial tradition, that they limit their disciples to the secular realm.[9]

Eric Voegelin has made this sort of complaint in the case of Jean-Paul Sartre, and what he says applies, *mutatis mutandis,* to the majority of feminist political philosophies:

> Take the case of Sartre's existentialism. He speaks of *la facticité de l'existence.* To analyse Sartre, I would start from that point: whether in classic philosophy or in Christianity existence is *not* a fact but always a tension in the openness toward something which is *more* than the fact of existence. Reality is always something else than the reality which is a fact. So with "existence is a fact," we have made a fundamentally fallacious interpretation of existence.[10]

CHRISTIAN REFLECTIONS II

A fundamentally true interpretation of existence pays special heed to human beings' openness toward something that is more than the fact of existence. Existence is a mystery, and human consciousness is in tension toward the divinity of that mystery, the creative fullness from which contingent existence derives and into which contingent existence returns. Not to honor this divine mystery is to build a flat roof over the human spirit, to deny it access to Dante's "love that moves the stars." It is to import the pathology of Bergson's "closed soul," cut off from the sources of light that ultimately matter most.

Political science, as classical philosophers such as Voegelin practice it, moves from such sources of light to a sobriety about human time. Looking at history with an unblinking eye, it sees that most people prefer the life of shadows, of passions and appetites, to the life of reason and *agape.* The homonoia, or likemindedness, on which friendship and genuine human community depend cannot flower in such circumstances. There needs must be a conversion to the elemental truths of human beings' radical equality under God, human beings' radical immersion in the biosphere, for a balanced, realistic, truly viable set of political orders to emerge.

If one follows the thread of women's liberation through these different political orders, from the family to the United Nations, one sees again and again that selfishness and self-ignorance bar the way to genuine prosperity. Husbands will not consider their wives equal to themselves, fully human and fully entitled just as they are, because (1) they have not been educated to this view, and (2) it demands that they sacrifice some of their present privileges. Nations will not fully enfranchise their women, fully draw them into the talent pool, because (1) they have not been educated to this view, and (2) those presently profiting from the unjust situation would have to sacrifice some of their (ill-gotten) privileges.

Soberly seen, therefore, any significant social movement reveals the depths of disorder in which the human race wallows. The movement for economic justice to members of the Third World soon leads to the realization that we need a new international economic system, based on the principle that no nation has the right to abuse another nation's labor or resources. The movement for racial justice soon leads to the realization that peoples of color suffer such a pervasive shortchanging that only a great cultural leap forward could ever give them parity. The most compassionate reading of the secular philosophies' failure to deal adequately with the basic problems of human meaning attributes that failure to exhaustion before the immensity of the task. It were well, then, for us women to measure the liberation issue accurately, lest we embark on it unaware of its full implications. The inner logic of liberation moves one relentlessly toward the Pauline new creation. There is no stopping for long at any way-station, no saying that any partial justice is enough. Full justice is the only place the true liberationist can rest, and realizing this makes her *Ausländer* to most of her peers.

In Christian terms, I am asking for a sober recognition of pilgrimage. To face feminist or any other profound social issues seriously, is to have "here" no lasting city. Whether dramatically or unobtrusively, the liberationist becomes a sort of *sannyasin,* wandering the world in search of final deliverance. A fine way to do this, of course, is to labor for justice as best one can here and now. That is how prophecy and pilgrimage can become practical. In this household, this workplace, this neighborhood, this church, I shall do what I can to let a better way emerge. It must be a way of peace, joy, and inner conviction. It must be a way of love and gentleness that nourishes me, makes me myself, with all my obvious imperfections, the first advertisement for my cause. The saints the polis needs in the future I foresee are the legions of men and women who simply *do* the deeds of justice, sexual equality, and love.

For example, welcomed or not, they form nonsexist religious groups, whether new churches or cadres within established churches, in which women pray, lead, speak, listen, in strict equality with men. They use a language that bespeaks the femininity of God as much as the masculinity, the divinity of women as much as men. So, too, in their places of work. Insofar as it depends upon them, they make their places of work zones where women get equal pay, equal responsibility, equal training, equal opportunity.

The families on which my future most depends are those similarly practical. Without a lot of talk, with considerable good humor and flexibility, they bind spouses and children to the proposition that time is for creative work, service, prayer, and play that blesses God. Weekends are not made for Michelob. Time is not given for mustering big bank accounts. What we eat, what we wear, what people think of us are of little consequence. Those are things after which heathen rush. We have a better calling.

Would that such a better calling would dominate our churches, synagogues, and schools. Would that they could become nakedly countercultural. Prizing the life of the mind, the life of the spirit, the life of service, they could show the polis how trashy its present aims are, moving it at least a smidgin toward a ministerial politics in which garbage removal, street paving, social work, and other public services are not the occupations of the despised but the occupations of strict equals. This might turn things a little toward the day when the consumer, the big house owner, the uncreative manager would have to justify his existence, rather than the little musician or art teacher. That is the politics I would like to see our reaching for justice, our future feminist partnership, develop.[11]

4/Ecology

CHAPTER SEVEN: CHRISTIAN THEOLOGY OF NATURE

A dimension of the future feminist partnership all too neglected in mainstream Christian theological circles is our immersion in the biosphere, the web of natural life. We humans are thoroughly ecological with physical creation, in ways whose subtlety we have only recently begun to suspect. True, women have sometimes intuited a special bond with nature, as the specimens of feminist writing on women's spiritual quest we saw above suggested. However, Christian theologians have seldom spent much time on the ecological dimensions of faith, largely because their anthropocentric interpretations of creation have so greatly subordinated physical nature to human culture.[1] Ecological spirituality therefore has been left to individual saints such as Francis of Assisi, who got along famously with brother sun and sister moon, and to the many simple rural folk who have loved God's disposition of the seasons.

To supplement the stripped, pilgrim life style hinted at the end of the last chapter, I would like to ponder the faithful "ecology" of some old Christians of New Mexico, caught by Robert Coles' tender prose near the close of their time. Here is an old Spanish woman speaking:

> "A few drops of rain and I feel grateful; the air is so fresh afterwards. I love to sit in the sun. We have the sun so often here, a regular visitor, a friend one can expect to see often and trust. I like to make tea for my husband and me. At midday we take our tea outside and sit on our bench, our backs against the wall of the house. Neither of us wants pillows; I tell my daughters and sons that they are soft—those beach chairs of theirs. Imagine beach chairs here in New Mexico, so far from any ocean! The bench feels strong to us, not uncomfortable. The tea warms us inside, the sun on the outside. I joke with my husband; I say we are part of the house; the adobe gets baked, and so do we. For the most part we say nothing, though. It is enough to sit and be part of God's world. We hear the birds talking to each other, and are grateful they come as close to us as they do; all the more reason to keep our tongues still and hold ourselves in one place."[2]

I hope this passage calls to mind Erikson's notion of wisdom, the virtue proper to old age, and also our prior discussion of contemplation. This old woman thinks on the end of things, as Coles' further narration more fully shows, and she prays to God from the heart, almost wordlessly. The point I would underscore now, though, is her connaturality with the rain, the sun, the air, and the birds. She is a citizen of God's world, for whom all that lives praises the Lord. She would surely applaud Augustine's notion that the species of subhuman creation are God's vestiges: footprints showing where He walked as He fashioned the world in love. There is little likelihood that this woman has studied ecology in a formal way. She says nothing about photosynthesis or water cycles. But nature is for her a genuine habitat, a niche where she feels at home. Unlike most urban dwellers, she still moves with the seasons, still rises with the sun and retires by the stars. A large part of her peace comes from the sense of proportion this gives her. In the broad vistas of New Mexico, her own life is small. The everlasting hills to which she lifts up her eyes make her earthly passage seem fleeting. Before long she will be at the end of her time to live, will reach her time to die.

So the life cycle prompts a certain ecological sensitivity, when our natural surroundings are favoring. The grandmother who taught the Appalachian woman Hannah the beauty of God's leaves was ripe like this New Mexican woman. Indeed, many aged people finally learn to live day by day, savoring time rather than rushing through it. As their bodies decline, they see the folly of most human bustle. T. S. Eliot pinpointed this folly when he spoke of having had the experience but having missed the meaning. We have all had the experience of living amidst a wondrous nature, but most of us have missed the meaning.

At the least, then, a Christian theology of nature has to make our bodies, through which we are ecological with the rest of creation, real and precious. At the least, it has to extend the Incarnation and the Sacraments to our nerves and bones. More ambitiously, such a theology might attend to women's somatic experience, trying to capitalize on our menstrual periodicity. Obviously enough, women are cyclic in ways men are not, even when fuller study of men's biological clocks shows them also running subtle patterns. The immemorial association of women with the moon taught tribal humanity that time was feminine. Like the moon (and mother earth), woman was ever in stately motion, ever passing from fallowness to fullness to fallowness again. Feminists are fully justified in resisting any tendency to make women's periodicity grounds for a biological determinism. A woman's imagination and brain determine more of her self than her hormones do. But feminists are also justified in seeking the spiritual implications of women's periodicity—their inner space, hormones, and sense of time.

For classical Chinese culture, the natural system that encompassed reality moved by feminine measures. The Tao was subtle, indirect, and nurturing. It preferred *wu-wei,* what Boulding might call gentle, passive-action, to *pa,* brutish force. And even the Confucians, the masters of male supremacy, honored this cosmic Tao, for from it irradiated a motherly love.[3] I have reflected elsewhere on the political side of Taoism's implications for feminists.[4] With the new witches, I would now like to see a motherly nature start to stimulate an ecological theology.

STEADY-STATE ECONOMICS

Of course, ecology is not a purely religious matter. It involves science, technology, politics, and economics. Indeed, so strong is the tendency of our culture to reduce complex questions like ecology to their economic aspect that books such as this must bend over backward to insist that ecology or environmentalism is a thoroughly religious and ethical issue. So doing, we run directly counter to the crass views of leading mavens like Lester Thurow:

> From this perspective, environmentalism is a natural product of a rising real standard of living. We have simply reached the point where, for many Americans, the next item on their acquisitive agenda is a cleaner environment. If they can achieve it, it will make all of the other goods and services (boats, summer homes, and so forth) more enjoyable. Environmentalism is not ethical values pitted against economic values. It is thoroughly economic. It is simply a case where a particular segment of the income distribution wants some economic goods and services (a clean environment) that cannot be achieved without collective action. Therefore, they have to persuade the rest of society that it is important to have a clean environment and impose rules and regulation that force others to produce a clean environment.[5]

Sorry, Lester, it's not as simple as that.

Fortunately, there are economists less crass, such as Herman Daly, who is willing to speak of "The Ecological and Moral Necessity of Limiting Economic Growth."[6] Daly puts aside the acquisitiveness of the upper middle class to concentrate on the scientific core of the issue, the limits of renewable resources. For, while nonrenewable resources such as oil and coal receive most attention:

> actually the more basic problem is with *renewable* resource systems and the destruction of their capacity to reproduce. A reduction in the sustainable yield capacity of a renewable resource system, such as forests, fisheries, grasslands, and croplands, is a far more serious matter than the depletion of a non-renewable resource. The latter is, after all, inevitable in the long run. The former is not inevitable (except in the astronomical long run). Any permanent reduction in renewable carrying capacity means fewer and/or less abundant lives will be lived in the future. This reduction should be minimized if we aspire to be good stewards of God's creation (p. 212).

Daly made these observations at the World Council of Church's 1979 Conference (held at the Massachusetts Institute of Technology) on Faith, Science and the Future. He focuses on the question of a sustainable economy, which lies at the heart of the issues of food, warfare, justice, and participatory political structures that occupied the Conference. With a lovely incisiveness, Daly sets the essential economic problem elegantly: to sustain an economy, one needs only a renewable resource base and a scale of population and consumption that does not exceed what that base can support. What worries him is that the per capita productivity of each of the four natural resource systems is on the decline. For example, forest productivity seems to have peaked in 1967, fisheries productivity to have peaked in 1970, grasslands productivity to have peaked for wool in 1960, mutton in 1972, and beef in 1976, and croplands productivity to have peaked in 1976.

To meet the implications of this situation responsibly, we human beings might define our biophysical budget and live within it. In effect, this would mean determining the level at which we can sustain production from the four renewable resource systems and not exceeding that level. That would be a responsible course of action, what one would expect creatures charged with the stewardship of creation to choose. The second option is to allow technology to keep increasing the total use, ignoring the limited biophysical budget. This is what the current growth economists suggest, and what the United States seems to be choosing to do; for example, by pursuing a policy of wilderness exploitation rather than a policy of wilderness preservation. Daly calls the choice for growth the response of "modern Promethean paganism."

Behind the first, stewardly choice lies an extension of the commandment, "Thou shalt not kill." Ecologically, this commandment has to mean, "Thou shalt not destroy the capacity of creation to support life." It is true, of course, that many representatives of Third World peoples oppose the stewardly option, since they think it means foreclosing their peoples' chances to gain a good life. Indeed, some of these representatives call the developed countries' ecological concern a matter of bad will—the fear of the affluent that they may lose their pampered life style.[7] This charge is another instance of reductionism, similar to Thurow's, but certainly more defensible. Unless the affluent countries couple their proposals for a steady-state world economy, or a world ecological policy that emphasizes restraint at the level of sustainable yield, with proposals for redistributing the world's wealth on a more equitable basis, the Third World countries have every right to suspect the affluent nations' intentions.

All of this, however, is rather academic, since the affluent countries show little inclination to give over an economics of maximum growth in favor of a steady-state economic philosophy. They are at least as far from this conversion as they are from redistributing the fruits of their growth economies so that the gulf between the rich nations and the poor nations might lessen rather than grow. Whether the issue be ecological stewardship or distributive justice, the affluent nations are so flagrantly greedy that any Christian theology mindful of the biblical prophets has to condemn them bitterly.

BIO-ETHICS

When the biblical prophets and their descendants condemn the profiteering of the rich on the poor, they cry out against an abuse of life. Simply by living, our fellow human beings have a right to justice. They are as much God's images as we, so there is a ground-level equality among us. On the basis of this ground-level equality, Christian ethicians traditionally proposed such maxims of social justice as, "No one has the right to superfluities so long as anyone lacks necessities." Condemning a view of private property that would vitiate God's having created the earth for all the earth's people, the fathers of the Church insisted that almsgiving, charity, and solicitude for the poor are duties, not matters of supererogation.

It is true that our current American economy cares for some of these duties, by taxing us for the support of government welfare agencies. It is not true that Christianity thereby sanctions a private enterprise that allows the wealthy to ride roughshod over the poor. Social Darwinism is not compatible with the gospel. Anyone who doubts the un-Christian character of right-wing capitalism should look again at Jesus' parabolic condemnation of those who ignore their poor neighbors (see Matt. 25 and Luke 16). One has to do somersaults to exclude from the fires of Gehenna all the corporation executives who prefer profits to their workers' health.

Ethically, then, ecology pushes forward the surpassing value of all life. Human life has a paramount value, of course, but plant and animal life also have rights. Indeed, as I shall argue at the end of the next chapter, simple be-ing evokes respect and reverent treatment, when human beings are genuinely religious. Simple quiet is a gift of God. Perhaps the advance corps of bio-ethicians, however, are those who link their concerns for being and life with the theses of liberation theology. Karen Lebacqz's essay, "Bio-ethics: Some Challenges from a Liberation Perspective,"[8] illustrates this movement.

Lebacqz begins her essay with the proposition that the predominant Western approach to bio-ethical issues suffers serious limitations. She therefore proposes to challenge this approach in the light of feminist and liberation trends. The present approach is characterized by such traits as (1) a decision orientation, focused on doing the right thing; (2) an individualistic orientation, focusing on the patient-physician relationship, rather than on such systemic issues as poor housing, inadequate sewerage, lack of access to health care, and the like; (3) an ahistorical mentality suffering from the misapprehension that once a "right" answer is found it will be correct for all similar cases; (4) a tendency to regard scientific evidence as normative, neglecting both the feelings of the people most intimately involved and the value-laden nature of all ethical data; and (5) a failure to *ground* the norms of bio-ethical decisions; for example, in specifically Christian virtues such as faith, hope, and love.

In contrast to these five problematic aspects of the prevailing Western bio-ethics, Lebacqz offers feminist and liberation insights that stress (1) patterns of meaning and structural concerns. For example, a recent conference run by women on ethical issues in reproductive technology changed the emphasis from questions such as whether *in vitro* fertilization is right or wrong, to questions such as "who holds the power to make such decisions, what the impact of all biomedical technologies combined is on the lives of women in this society, and so on" (p. 277). Beneath these questions lies the cultural issue of the biases of a given era, its myths and prejudices, which may seriously depreciate certain segments of the population, such as women. Such myths and prejudices play no small part in the elevation of male physicians to demigod status, and in the concomitant degradation of many women by gynecologists. From a feminist and liberationist point of view, the primary question of the new bio-ethical situation is what the dominant social structures are doing to the lives of the oppressed.

(2) In contrast to the individualistic orientation of the prevailing outlook, Lebacqz offers an orientation in terms of

story and community. This means that the individual's decision regarding (for example) abortion only makes full sense when it is placed in the pattern of her whole life, as well as in the pattern of her community, her society of belief. (3) This more social stress, in turn, argues for a historical approach, rather than the ahistorical notion that correct answers fall outside temporal relativities. One ought to ask, for instance, whether the new biomedical technologies should be developed in the absence of basic nutritional, health, and medical care in the Third World countries. Prescinding from history, one might argue that, since they hold out potential for good, we should develop the new biomedical technologies. Taking history into account, however, one might well argue that reasonable priorities now place the massive needs of the world's poor for elemental health care ahead of the somewhat esoteric health needs of the world's affluent.

(4) Again making links with the foregoing viewpoints, feminists argue that the *experience* of the people massively involved in health programs deserves high status, along with the scientific "facts." This results in questions that many establishmentarians never raise. For example, "What is the experience of women who want desperately to become pregnant and are unable to conceive? Why do they want this so desperately—i.e. what in the system creates this need?" (p. 280). (5) Feminists are also suggesting that we reconsider the traditional grounds for bio-ethics and broaden them, in order to admit such new grounds as the experience of oppression, women's bodily experiences, women's dreams, feminist rituals, and the like.

PROCESS VIEWS

Among the most prominent grounds for a Christian ecological ethics is God's act of creation. For those who see the world as a free overture of divine love, nothing in the world is despicable. Still, the Christian tradition has not done much for a reverent treatment of nonhuman creation. As John B. Cobb, Jr., a leading process theologian, puts it: "To any Christian concerned with the humane treatment of our fellow creatures, the record of Christian treatment is an embarrassment. Even today Christians generally side with humanists in arguing for thoroughly anthropocentric positions."[9] Process theologians, who largely derive their views fom the work of Alfred North Whitehead, challenge these anthropocentric positions. For them, human beings are much more immersed in the evolutionary process than traditional Christian theologians have appreciated. Indeed, God herself is ecological with the rest of creation, having in her "consequent nature" a thorough identification with the world.[10]

From its sense of the interconnectedness of all creatures, process theology would raise the sense of participation in nature that human beings should have. Thus Cobb and David Griffin say in their *Process Theology:*

> Process theology calls for still further extension of the sense of participation. The whole of nature participates in us and we in it. We are diminished not only by the misery of the Indian peasant but also by the slaughter of whales and porpoises, and even by the "harvesting" of giant redwoods. We are diminished still more when the imposition of temperate-zone technology onto tropical agriculture turns grasslands into desert that will support neither human nor animal life.[11]

Participation therefore is a call to think in terms of the whole. No section of the natural world exists apart from the others; the welfare of one relates to the welfare of all. It was easier to neglect this truth in the days when our technologies were not so lethal. Today it is frighteningly clear that our air, water, land, and animal life interact with us so intimately that the pollution of these fellow creatures brings pollution into our own bodies.

This is not to say that we should only insist on clear air, water, and land because our own lungs, blood, and bones are at stake. Beyond such personal interest lies the more ontological demand that we not kill the life-carrying capacity of the planet, not abuse anything that has come to be (especially anything we ourselves have not created). Opposing the hubris of strip mining, wanton offshore drilling, and chemical fouling of the rivers is a simple sense of religion that tribal peoples usually manifested better than we. Everything that is, is holy, simply because it is. We have no more right to deface the landscape than we have to deface our neighbor's home, the windows of the bank downtown, or the cement newly laid in the park.

People who deface things lack a gene or a basic unit of human education. They are careless, irresponsible, in ways that cry to heaven for redress. For the things that exist are items we hold in trust. When we tear pages from library books, trample a school's flowers, or litter a parking lot with beer bottles, we show ourselves to be criminally underdeveloped. It is a much more serious matter to poison the land with radiation or chemicals, of course, but it is in the same pattern of irresponsibility. Either because of carelessness or greed, very many human beings ab-use creation. In any adequate theology, such people forfeit their rights to enjoy nature's fruits.

Were a process view of creation to impress itself more deeply on Christianity, more theologians might, like John Cobb, expend themselves generously on behalf of ecological issues.[12] They could add another level of reflection to that of the naturalists, such as Annie Dillard and Lewis Thomas,[13] who expose the poetry of our participation in an ecological world. The full thrust of such theological reflection, I suspect, would go in the direction of a much simpler life style than what the American churches now propose to their constituents. Specifically, the thrust probably would include a much more conserving attitude toward energy and natural resources. We American Christians are a wasteful people, sinfully so in the spectrum of the world's hunger and poverty. Our per capita use of resources is so many times that of an Indian or Latin American that we unwittingly separate ourselves from them into a private history, a thin time-line for the wealthy. But who so preaches "participation" from the pulpit that, in the name of Christian theology, people hear a call to foreswear these foolish ways? Who speaks seriously of small housing units, vegetarian diets, a life style based on spiritual culture rather than material consumption? In the future I would like to see feminist Christian theologians who would speak of these things eloquently.

I might illustrate the general state of affairs with an example that has especially disturbed me, even though I have only encountered it from afar, through the newspapers. It is the decision to allow offshore drilling for oil at Georges Bank in the North Atlantic. Georges Bank is one of the prime fishing areas in the world. It is an inestimable food resource, as well as the place from which thousands of fishermen draw their livelihood. In our country's insatiable demand for more oil, we have chosen to endanger Georges Bank (since the chances of a damaging oil spill are bound to be high). I realize that I am neither a marine biologist nor a petroleum engineer, so there are huge aspects of this example that lie outside my competence. Nonetheless, I do not have much doubt in my bones that this is a bad, unethical, un-Christian decision, abjuring our responsibility to husband the sea and pandering to our people's prodigal greed. We would rather ruin Georges Bank than drive 55 miles an hour.

FEMINIST REFLECTIONS I

No doubt there would be debate in feminist circles as to whether women should have to carry the full baggage of a stripped life style, a steady-state economy, a conservationist love of the sea, and the like in order to qualify for full membership in "the movement." In a time when the Equal Rights Amendment is under a cloud, the full agenda of an "Ecotopia"[14] may seem irresponsibly broad. Nonetheless, as the Whiteheadean notion of "prehension" reminds us, things relate to other things, sharing existence ecologically, whether we like it or not. Therefore, even when we limit ourselves practically or politically, so as to use our energies most efficiently, we must stay aware of the connections that make feminism a natural ally of other movements for justice, other defenses of life.

However, support for a stripped life style seems to come rather naturally to people who work with ecological and demographic issues, as some almost offhand remarks of Donella Meadows suggest. Meadows received a doctorate in biophysics from Harvard, worked as a research associate in the Department of Nutrition at MIT, and with her husband Dennis wrote the famous Club of Rome computer study, *Limits to Growth.* In 1975 she returned to her alma mater, Carleton College, to participate in a symposium later published as *Finite Resources and the Human Future.*[15] At this symposium she had the following to say about a steady-state domestic life: "The everyday institutions—the family and the business and the educational institutions, and the way you work and the way you play—will be different in the steady-state world. . . . It may be that the nuclear family is not right, nor the old extended family. Something different may be right; some sort of communal arrangement, especially since there will not be many children" (p. 123).

Meadows is quick to point out that her life style may not fit everyone. She may have changed her mind about having children, and today many aspects of the whole symposium suggest the idealism of a lost era, when "alternate life styles" still mustered a surge of enthusiasm. The problem with writing alternate life styles off, though, is that the ecological facts that originally prompted them have lost none of their cogency. Things may change temporarily in such areas as oil distribution, but the massive problems of energy production, food production and distribution, and population control remain very much with us. Even if an electorate forgets these global facts, demanding from its leaders a still higher material standard of living, the biophysical realities remain.

Nicolas Georgescu-Roegen has illustrated these realities

vividly: "Every time we produce a Cadillac, we do it at the cost of decreasing the number of human lives in the future. Economic development may be a blessing for us now and for those who will be able to enjoy it in the near future, but it is definitely against the interest of the human species as a whole, if its interest is to have a lifespan as long as is compatible with its dowry of low entropy."[16]

Popular or not, I would like to have feminism associate itself with the turn from expansionist economics to steady-state economics, the turn from consumerist life styles to life styles more ecologically conserving. The core reason is my belief that feminism, like healthy religion, places human prosperity in qualitative, spiritual relationships, rather than in material possessions. Obviously, I do not mean lecturing the poor on the sustenances of poetry. I do mean seeing the connections among the subspecies of the current Western ways of death. The military, industrial, banking, and other establishments that men now dominate fit together into an aggressive, competitive, consumerist, and lethal whole. These establishments bring some benefits, but their deficiencies are so glaring that common sense forces us to reexamine them critically. As women traditionally have played a large part in food production, and as their breast feeding continues to be the method best controlling worldwide population today,[17] so women's intellectual perception of the stripped life styles that would best nourish the global human family in the future, and best offset the current Western ways of death, is the best force for tipping the scales toward survival in the future.

This means a new feminine mystique, predicated on women's active delineation of the world in which they, the prime bearers of life, want future life to thrive. By their votes, their money, their manifold influences, formal and informal, a large corps of women dedicated to ecological sanity, social justice, and simple living could be the decisive factor in Mother Earth's preservation. Where such feminists might especially distinguish themselves, and join with the best people from the world's traditional religions, is in hallowing the words "self-sacrifice" and "service." Properly understood, those words—I say this sadly—are the last defense against a world wholly given over to profit and power.

FEMINIST REFLECTIONS II

High on the list of professional women who deserve well of both feminists and Christians for having made self-sacrifice and service eminently practical stands the late Barbara Ward, economist, internationalist, and ecologist. Lady Jackson, as she was known in titled circles, resolutely championed the poor, working with United Nations commissions to show very specific ways in which a more just international order might begin to emerge. Ward attacked the full range of economic issues in one of her last books, *Progress for a Small Planet,*[18] but she gave agriculture a special priority. Perhaps, then, agriculture should be one of the ecological foci on which women concentrate.

In Ward's view, agriculture offers the clearest clues, or best shows the decisive steps, in the process whereby the developed countries became modernized. A key time and place, for example, was mid-eighteenth century Britain, which not only saw the building of the steam engine and the inventing of coking coal, but also saw the introduction of the fourfold rotation of crops, the use of the turnip as winter feed for cattle, and marling (primitive fertilizing). These technical advances provided a surplus of food and rural wealth that country bankers and entrepreneurs could tap; in order, for example, to turn rural Lancaster into the base for a new cotton industry. However, one of the dark sides to this development was the loss to the landless of the right to glean and to keep their animals on what had been communal lands.

> They were part of the growing proletariat thrust into the unspeakable miseries of the new industrial cities or forced to

> distant exile in the New World. The effects were in some ways comparable to the dispossession of the rural poor being brought about in the developing world by today's "Green Revolution"—with big machines, new seeds, artificial fertilizers, and increasing output for the well-to-do farmers, but a steady shedding of manpower in the process. Britain's sufferings were probably less than today's evils (pp. 173-74).

Even when one passes over the likely analogies to United States agriculture, where part of the pattern is for large-scale growers and conglomerates to force family farmers out, Ward's point of view should impress American feminists. She has a special interest in the plight of those whom "progress" displaces, an interest that mainline economists and businessmen frequently do not have. Thus implicit in her reference to the Green Revolution is a call to evaluate it holistically. Against the gains that such technologies hold out we must weigh not only the strictly ecological factors such as how one fertilizes the soil to gain the new seeds' greater yield, but also the social factors such as the human suffering entailed. I think there is a good chance that only a massive infusion of women into agricultural economics would bring it about that human sufferings became a regular part of the "efficiency" calculus. I say this not because I think women have a gene for sanctity, or because I think women trained to academic economics cannot be co-opted by its supposed toughmindedness, but rather in the spirit of Elise Boulding, looking to history's marginal people for ways out of our current economic patterns of insensitivity.

Ward goes on to add similar humanistic nuances that, almost in passing, give her work a feminist sensitivity. Thus she notes that, in assessing the primacy of successful agriculture in the Western nations' march to modernization, we must recall how the colonial powers repressed the "backward" nations' local industries: "It was widely believed—and not without cause—that colonial powers had either actually impeded or at least not encouraged local industrial processes that would compete with their own. The Indians compared their struggles against Lancashire—which insisted on countervailing duties on Indian textiles—with the genuine 'giant leap forward' of independent Japan's textile industry at the turn of the last century" (p. 175). She also notes the almost accidental advantage that North America had, because of the mass of its arable land compared with its small number of farmers available to work the land. Whereas there were only about five million Americans in 1780, both India and China had more than 100 million inhabitants. Add this to the American access to European developments in husbandry, and to the Baconian atmosphere of confidence and exploitation, and you have explained a great many of the differences in what the nineteenth century brought to North America, in contrast to India and China.

Why should all this agricultural economics interest the feminist? It shouldn't, unless she agrees with Ward that the prime aim of society is to conserve people (rather than increase the GNP).

> Three quarters of the people in the developing world (more than 2 billion) live in rural areas. Even in the middle-income states, where growth rates of over 5 percent were maintained in the fifties and sixties, the growing wealth all too often failed to reach the countryside. It is there, among the farm people . . . that is to be found 80 percent of the world's "absolute poverty," with malnutrition, high mortality, crippling disease, illiteracy, and lack of work (p. 177).

Moreover, since these poor people have the world's highest birth rates, over 40 percent of them are less than fifteen years old. They may receive some help, if experiments in new forms of rural organization that the modernizing nations have tried are extended. On the average, however, only 20 percent of the investments of most developing nations has gone to the 70 or 80 percent of the people who live in the rural areas. I would like to have feminists seeking to reverse trends such as these; for example, by arguing that a people's political usefulness to our developed countries should not be the determining factor in whether we help them get a chance to lead truly human lives.

CHAPTER EIGHT: FEMINIST THEORY OF NATURE

If the Christian theology of nature needs to develop the venerable character of the physical world, linking this to the imperatives for ecological care, spare living, and the service of the world's malnourished that we sketched in the last chapter, a feminist theory of nature needs to make the physical world a congenial habitat for women and tie this ecology to the economics, politics, and other aspects of the new order women hunger to bring forth. At the outset of the last chapter we contemplated an aged New Mexican woman, enjoying her enjoyment of a warm sun, a gentle breeze, a few drops of rain, and birds chirping happily. Projecting from experiences like this, Doris Lessing has filled her *Canopus in Argos* with descriptions of flora, fauna, and architecture that emphasize the importance of our *environment.* For both health and sickness, the importance of our surroundings is hard to exaggerate. This can give a new wrinkle to the old theme of women's concern with design and decoration.

Consider, for example, Lessing's description of one of the cities of Rohanda, the planet Earth now in a period of decline. Early in *Shikasta*[1] she writes:

> I did not want this journey to end. Oh, what a lovely place was the old Rohanda! Never have I found, not in all my travelings and visitings, a more pleasant land, one that greeted you so softly and easily, bringing you into itself, charming, beguiling, so that you had to succumb, as one does to the utterly amazing charm of a smile or a laugh that seems to say, "Surprised, are you? Yes, I am

extra, a gift, superfluous to the necessary, a proof of the generosity concealed in everything" (p. 30).

"The generosity concealed in everything": creation and manufacture conspiring to make life graceful, a series of *dona superaddita* (extras).

I think of Rohanda wistfully after visiting downtown (which is no more noisy, acrid, or ugly in my city than in most others). I think of the Round City:

> The Round City showed nothing that was not round. It was a perfect circle, and could not expand: its bounds were what had to be. The outer walls of the outer buildings made the circle, and the side walls, as I made my way through on a path that was an arc, I saw were slightly curved. The roofs were not flat, but all domes and cupolas, and their colours were delicate pastel shades, creams, light pinks and soft blues, yellows and greens, and these glowed under the sunny sky . . . [it] was thronged, and a healthier friendlier crowd I have never seen. A pervasive good humour was the note of this place, amiability—and yet it was not clamorous or hectic. And I noted that despite the noise a crowd must produce, this did not impinge on the deep silence that was the ground note of this place, the music in its inner self, which held the whole city safe in its harmonies (pp. 31-32).

Lessing is writing apocalyptic: visionary stuff about the time of crisis, when a civilization's weaknesses will show as rippling faults and its strengths will be proven through endurance. The Round City is on the verge of losing its harmonies, but its sources of order—its architecture, silence, and music—preserve it far longer than places less well designed would survive. This is but one graphic from the novel's full-scale design, but we must not miss the meaning. Our architecture, homes, music, sculpting of nature, and the like tell what is in our souls.

That is an obverse, quite apparent meaning. The reverse, more subtle meaning is that our architecture, homes, music, sculptings of nature, and the like, shape our souls. We are how we dwell, what we sing, even more than what we eat. Our atmosphere, the milieu we create, tells the trained observer almost too much about our spirits. One of the worst discoveries I made on a trip around the world in 1976 was that North America was the leader in pollution control. From Europe to India to Japan, the rest of the world was even more careless about smog and noise.

However, let me so associate myself with Lessing's full apocalypse that I avoid the charge of aestheticism. Her entire work certainly absolves her of this charge, for it is eminently concerned with war, politics, and the other matters our time deems more serious than aesthetics. Still, I insist that we neglect our milieu at our peril. This shows in small matters: the woman next door who screams at her kids like a fishwife already finds them screaming back. She is thirty years old, forty pounds overweight, and married to a man who seems mainly to test loud engines. Together they have the good life: three times the room they need, four times the horsepower, twice the calories, and perhaps a quarter of the intellectual stimulation. They are middle America, the unattractive half. In great matters, one need only regard the air of our cities, the caliber of our entertainment, the aesthetics of our tract housing, the speech of our politicians.

Small and great, the matters of our environment, our human ecological niche, still tend to drive the serious, the sensitive, the lovers of beauty into the desert, as established Christianity did in the fourth century. So perhaps things were ever thus. On the other hand, one catches glimpses they were not (as one catches glimpses in current America that some people still have souls). For example, C. G. Jung sat with the Indian Ochwiay Biano on the roof of his pueblo, watching the blazing sun rise higher and higher. Biano was immersed in the blue sky, the golden light, utterly silent. Finally there broke from him the exclamation: "How can there be another god? Nothing can be without the sun."[2] His atmosphere, the milieu his people shaped, was not a prop for distraction.

NATURE AND CULTURE

Much of the recent reflection on women's place in what we might call "environmental design" can lead to the anthropological question of the relation between nature and culture. My impression, unfortunately, is that many of the writings on this question throw little light on what I take to be the aesthetico-politico-religious core. For instance, while I sympathize with Susan Griffin's desire in *Woman and Nature*[3] to probe the insight that "men consider women to be more material than themselves, or more a part of nature" (p. xv), I find her associative style leaving the logic of this insight more obscured than revealed. Sherry Ortner's view[4] that most societies consider nature inferior to culture, because culture works to transform nature, would indeed seem to play a role in the subordination of women (insofar as a society contrasts women's natural creativity with men's cultural creativity), but other anthropologists have somewhat questioned this thesis,[5] and world-views such as Saigyo's Japanese Buddhism[6] call it into question completely, by positing nature as superior to culture. To be sure, Ortner did not say that most societies simply equate women with nature. But she did find women tending to be considered closer to nature than men, and so tending more than men to mediate between nature and culture.

I'd like to probe this characterization briefly, ruminating on whether it can't be turned to feminist account. First, granted that many societies have used women's natural fertility to distinguish their social contribution from men's,[7] some societies certainly have so revered nature that this distinction became a source of women's prestige. Second, in other societies, such as those of the modern West, in which human invention made men think they dominated the rest of evolution, women may indeed have been the losers, as supposedly "higher" creativity passed into male hands. Then women dominated primary education while men dominated universities, women adjudicated domestic squabbles while men passed judgment at the bar. The

Victorian association of business and politics with the "dirty" but "real" world of money and power led to the trivialization of women, as we saw, and that in turn helped the mechanistic science, technology, and entrepreneurship of the late nineteenth and early twentieth centuries to disregard the feminine and the mysterious.

Things appear to be different today, at least in sophisticated circles. Whereas we used to ravish nature rather unthinkingly, some of us now realize there is an ecological crisis. Whereas we used to think of military and political affairs in terms of *Realpolitik,* some of us now realize that people (such as the Vietnamese, Iranians, and Arabs) have to be *persuaded* (as Plato could have taught us long ago).

Of course persuasion is a two-edged sword, as experts from Madison Avenue to Communist "reeducation" camps remind us. But granted a will to justice rather than a will to power, persuasion becomes the art of alluring people with truth's beauty (much as the Whiteheadean God lures creation forward). Like the new ecological science, which would only interfere in nature delicately, the new politics of persuasion would seem a feminine art. Reflecting the cosmic Tao, which moves by *wu-wei* ("not-doing"), it is more subtle, more playful, more profound; in a word, more human than the ways we have lately called realistic.

So, I would take it as at least a potential badge of honor to be considered closer to nature than to (the prevailing) culture. Early in any discussion I would affirm that, as a woman, I am neither more natural nor less cultured than a comparable man, but I would not let the denigration of nature slip by unchallenged. Hundreds of thousands of scientists make their living and consecrate their time by studying nature. After hundreds of years, astronomers have more questions than they have answers, as do atomic physicists. "Nature" is more than a match for culture. The Logos who moves through the universe, grounding its entelechies, is worthy of great honor, glory, and devotion.

So, if we women historically have been the more natural sex, through our child-bearing (and perhaps also through our discovery of agriculture), we should not lightly cast over this association today, when so many human needs boil down to finding a more natural way of proceeding. Assuming the association does not deny women's many historical and symbolic relations to culture (recall all the Goddesses, from a great variety of cultural pools, who are patronesses of the arts, sciences, and social skills), it would seem to be something to exploit in a mood of nurturing.

Doing so, we might advance such movements as holistic medicine, in which the patient's physical environment, emotions, exercise, diet, and peace of soul could all enter into the diagnosis. Similarly, we might help a smaller-scale farming emerge, giving more people the chance to leave the noise and grime of the cities, and helping the nation with a higher per-acre yield. Countless other areas of the economy might profit from a more labor-intensive approach, were we willing to treat the land and its raw materials more gently. Countless other places of work might prosper, were we willing to give higher priority to furnishing workers a pleasant environment. These would all be steps toward a "Buddhist" (Feminist) economics, in which people mattered more than profits.

I do not oppose decent profits, any more than I oppose controlled high technology or necessary forms of military violence. Each of these aspects of our current culture has its place. I do oppose the relatively unbridled influence that profits, high technology, and military violence now seem to exert. It is hard not to believe that they run us more than we run them. Is that not a rather ironic result for a "rational," male-dominated culture to produce? Should it not lead the fair-minded to consider a more natural, feminist approach, in which disarmament, ecological preservation, and an economy serving all the people as justly as possible were the aims? Mediating between physical nature and this sort of human culture, women would be laboring at nothing less than soteriology—nothing less than the race's deepest nursing.

NATURE, CULTURE, AND THE ANCHORITE

I noted earlier how the crass aspects of current American culture tend to drive sensitive souls into the "desert," for healing and strengthening. This is another submotif playing through my ponderings about nature and culture. Sometimes truly cultivated persons come to their best perceptions while on retreat from urban culture. Often the desert or the woods or the sea frames new insights into the gyrations of the madding crowd. This proved true for Annie Dillard. Though her *Pilgrim at Tinker Creek*[8] concerned itself focally with the wonders of the Virginia woods, it never left the madding crowd very far behind. Perhaps reviewing some of the things Dillard learned about nature's *fecundity,* and so facing the fuller significance of women's ties to nature, would bring our own crowds into better focus.

Dillard begins her meditation on fecundity by describing a nightmare she suffered, in which fisheggs hatched and covered her bed with a viscid slime. Then she moves to the reflective level: "I don't know what it is about fecundity that so appalls. I suppose it is the teeming evidence that birth and growth, which we value, are ubiquitous and blind, that life itself is so astonishingly cheap, that nature is as careless as it is bountiful, and that with extravagance goes a crushing waste that will one day include our own cheap lives . . ." (p. 160). In this sober mood, nature's fecundity becomes hellish (making human culture more heavenly?). Let us take up this devil's advocacy, for it will temper any romanticism in our ecological aesthetic.

The plant world does not seem to make fecundity hellish. An acre of poppies or a forest of spruce does not appall. (It does, however, betray a prodigality few of us ever appreciate: in four months a single plant of winter rye can send forth 378 miles of roots, in 14 million distinct roots. The roots can create 14 billion root hairs, the length of which in a single cubic inch of soil can reach 6000 miles). But the constant reproduction of animal life does somehow seem appalling, at least to a poet such as Annie Dillard. For example, the barnacles encrusting a single half mile of shore can leak into the water a million million larvae. "What if God has the same affectionate disregard for us that we have for barnacles? I don't know if each barnacle larva is of itself unique and special, or if we the people are essentially as interchangeable as bricks" (p. 167).

So with much of the rest of the lower animal world. A lone aphid, breeding unmolested for a year, would produce enough offspring (each a tenth of an inch long) to reach twenty-five-hundred light years into space. This scale of breeding is only contained, monstrously enough, by the proclivity of parents and other predators to devour offspring in almost equally prodigal numbers. Thus a female lacewing laying her eggs atop a green leaf may pause to satisfy her hunger by eating the eggs as quickly as she produces them. Insofar as thousands of species repeat this pattern, it raises the possibility of a creation in love with death, wantonly destroying with the left hand as it creates with the right. In such a creation, we humans, who have emotions about these things, would be the freaks.

To lighten the tension of facing nature with highly pitched human emotions, Dillard shies away from "culture":

> I could use some calming down, and the creek is just the place for it. I must go down to the creek again. It is where I belong, although as I become closer to it, my fellows appear more and more freakish, and my home in the library more and more limited. Imperceptibly at first, and now consciously, I shy away from the arts, from the human emotional stew. I read what the men with telescopes and microscopes have to say about the landscape. I read about the polar ice, and I drive myself deeper and deeper into exile from my own kind. But, since I cannot avoid the library altogether—the human culture that taught me to speak in its tongue—I bring human values to the creek, and so save myself from being brutalized (pp. 178-79).

For the human being, then, nature and culture are kaleidoscopic, shifting constantly in different combinations. The sordidness or rank evil in culture that drives one to the anchoritic life has analogues in the apparent cruelty of nature, nature's careless dispensings of death. Shiva, the Lord of the Dance of Life, is also the Destroyer, the one who sets life in polar relation to death. Far from the disquieting crowd one finds a nature that calls for a theodicy almost as strongly as human history does. In the desert as well as the city, the world God has chosen to make can seem diabolically heartless. Then all our scenarios for a human ecology, a feminist politics of persuasion, a holistic culture Lao Tzu might approve can come crashing down, dashed on the rocks of death, evil, the surd so close to creation's core. No wonder the Taoist sage is ruthless, seeing the people as but straw dogs. He merely reflects Heaven and Earth, to which the ten thousand things are but as straw dogs.[9]

I am forced, therefore, to qualify the "naturalism" I would have feminists embrace. Feminists may move subtly, by persuasion rather than force, imitating water and the Tao, but I would not have them be ruthless. For all the wisdom in naturalist philosophy that lets go of human emotionalism in order to embrace the cosmic scale, I find something more precious in Christian revelation. That something is Christ's cross, taken as God's declaration that divinity is not indifferent to suffering. If the man Jesus spoke with a special authority, if his *agape* opened a new Kingdom, then God somehow loves the world through all the world's suffering, somehow brings resurrection where there may seem to be only death. Very theological, these anchoritic musings on nature and culture.

THE NUCLEAR THREAT

More horrible than the wantonness of lower animal life, which seems fecund with destruction, is the potential for evil latent in nuclear power. Whatever theodicy aphids might demand pales in the face of thermonuclear explosives. Taken as part of the ecological crisis, nuclear energy concentrates our greatest challenge. We have loosed a mad genie from the bottle, and it is far from clear we will get it back. In addition to the problems posed by the developed nations' thermonuclear weapons, we must control the spread of thermonuclear capacity to the developing nations, and we must also control the radiation hazards of our nuclear power plants. Many voices have taken up these cries, but few more effectively than that of Helen Caldicott, physician and mother.

Caldicott's *Nuclear Madness*[10] is a primer on both scientific information and practical tactics. It issues from her successful efforts to force the French to stop atmospheric testing in the South Pacific, and from her work to educate labor unions of her native Australia to the dangers of uranium. Like most books of this sort, *Nuclear Madness* abounds in mind-boggling statistics:

> A hydrogen bomb works on the fusion principle, the same process that fuels the sun. In such a bomb, the atoms in 1,000 tons of lithium deuteride are joined two at a time to form atoms of helium. In the process, enormous concussive force and thermal energy are released. The high temperature needed to get the process going is provided by an atom bomb, which serves as a triggering mechanism, releasing more than 15 million degrees of heat. A thousand times more powerful than an atom bomb, one hydrogen bomb can kill millions of people within seconds (pp. 78-79).

The United States has more than 11,894 strategic warheads in its arsenal, while the Soviet Union has more than 4,396. The United States has more than 20,000 tactical nuclear weapons, while the Soviet Union has more than 10,000. In 1978 the developed nations spent twenty times more for their military programs than they did for economic aid to poorer countries. In two days the world spends on arms what it allots the United Nations for a year. Although more than 1.5 billion people lack access to professional health services, and over 1.4 billion have no safe drinking water, and over 500 million suffer from malnutrition, world governments spend twice as much on arms as they do on health care.

Among the developing nations, the importation of sophisticated conventional arms exceeds $6 billion per year, although more than 700 million adults are illiterate and more than 500 million children (more than half) do not attend school. Military research, worldwide, occupies more than 500,000 scientists and engineers, and it receives more public funds than all social needs combined. Over half the scientists in the United States work for the military-industrial complex, and energy research and development receive only about one-sixth the funding of weapons research.

What is the goal of all this weapons research and expenditure? What will happen if all this money and labor come to fruition? "Each [nuclear] weapon's powerful shock wave would be accompanied by a searing fireball with a surface temperature greater than the sun's that would set firestorms raging over millions of acres. (Every 20 megaton bomb can set a firestorm raging over 3,000 acres. A 1,000 megaton bomb exploded in outer space could devastate an area the size of six western states)" (p. 81). The fires from nuclear explosions would consume great amounts of plant and wild life. The heat released in a full-scale war might melt the polar ice caps, flooding much of the planet. The earth's atmospheric ozone layer could be destroyed, resulting in serious hazards from cosmic and ultraviolet radiation.

The long-term effect on human beings (prescinding from the massive numbers of outright deaths) would likely include cancer epidemics. Within five years leukemia would be rampant; within fifteen to fifty years solid cancers of the breast, stomach, lung, bowel, and other organs would kill a large fraction. Many of the exposed would be rendered sterile, while many women would suffer spontaneous abortions and deformed offspring. The genetic mutations would be incalculable. Granted the interconnection of the ecological systems of the winds, waters, and worldwide food resources, there is a good chance that all human life, even that far outside the attack areas, would finally be imperiled.

Caldicott provides similarly gruesome statistics and pictures for such related problems as nuclear sewage, radiation, and the control of plutonium. Her perspective is medical as well as peace-making, for she has specialized in radiological work with children. Even were we human beings possessed of the most benign motives and political systems, nuclear energy would pose tremendous hazards. Granted the current state of international affairs, we are toying with racial destruction.

These are realities whose horror the mind almost refuses to admit. In addition, we have all grown suspicious of statistics, and weary of perfervid rhetoric. But the bare facts don't change. We store massive amounts of deadly force. We develop and deploy powers we do not know how to sanitize. For the money, the power, the hubris involved, our military-industrial complex keeps escalating the nightmare. How much of this horrible scenario comes from macho pride? Why not admit a huge mistake and call the whole thing off: deactivate the power plants, destroy the bombs, on each side? Great problems of radiation control would remain. There would be economic and diplomatic relocations. But we could do it, if we really wanted to. We could see the two ways set before us this day, the way of life and the way of death, and we could choose life.

CHRISTIAN REFLECTIONS I

By this juncture, I am happy to find, the lines between my "feminist" reflections and my "Christian" reflections have blurred. The areas of agreement I had hoped to discover have emerged rather spontaneously, often in terms of a common concern for "life." Thus the figure that seemed most appropriate for ending a feminist section on nuclear perils came from the Bible. I almost forgot to wonder how many potential fellow travelers such crossing-over might alienate, so natural did it seem.

In deciding now to discuss abortion, I wonder how much I

shall disturb such harmony between the two lobes of my mind-set. Unfortunately, the topic seems unavoidable, as the topic of nuclear power did, if we are to consider "ecology" in the depth and breadth it deserves. Still, I dread the topic, because it raises so much tempest, and because, even when one cuts away the rhetorical excesses, it is tempest in the soul, not in a teapot. I find women crossing feminist/Christian lines on the abortion issue, but most secular feminists still seem to champion abortion while most Christians would at best allow it. Once again, many factors are involved: economic, psychological, medical, theological, legal, and political. I wish to say only enough to fulfill the obligations I assumed when I set out to be somewhat comprehensive.

First, I think there is a pressing need, worldwide, for population control, and I have little patience with religious or (less frequently) ethnic/racial groups that do not plan their families in the light of the global situation. Second, while "natural," or at least non-chemical, means of contraception seem to me the wisest, I also have no patience with distinctions, such as the Roman Catholic, that make most means of contraception "artificial," and so, immoral. Even granting good will in the people who propose this view, I find it utterly unpersuasive.

Third, we had best realize that abortion tends, in practice, to be the "cure" to which the world's lower socio-economic levels of people most frequently resort, and that, overall, abortion probably is the third most popular form of population control:

> When a population is first exposed to medicine it tends to *curative* medication for a disease already incurred before it accepts the more sophisticated concept of *preventive* medication for a disease that it may never get. The same generalization applies to fertility control, with the "disease" being equated to an unwanted pregnancy. Here, the only "cure" is abortion. It is not surprising then that at the lower socioeconomic-cultural levels . . . where populations have not generally been exposed to preventive

> medicine, curative birth control is implemented first, and this accounts for the high incidence of abortion. Indeed, after the Pill and prolonged lactation, abortion is the most widely practiced form of birth control in the world today.[11]

About eight percent of the world's fertile women now have abortions in a given year,[12] and since the late 1830s, abortion has been a serious option for American women.[13]

Fourth, pluralistic societies such as our own have a serious political problem in accommodating the strong oppositions among their citizens that volatile issues such as abortion tend to raise. Legally and politically, the only way I can see out of the dilemma is to treat abortion as a matter on which persons of good will can disagree (i.e., not equate it with intrinsic evils such as murder), and then to exert the usual conscientious efforts to balance the will of the majority against the rights of the minorities. Thus an absolute prohibition against abortions would be unthinkable, but if the majority of citizens did not want their taxes to support abortions, because they considered abortions evil, government support of abortions could stop, leaving the matter to private agencics.

Fifth, the core moral issue is the nightmare, at least for me. On the one side, I am persuaded by the arguments that there will always be abortions, legal or not, and that poor women bear special burdens, including many threats to life, when restrictive abortion policies obtain. On the other side, my own instincts for peace rather than war, ecological preservation rather than pollution, and the nurture of life rather than life's threatening by violence cause me to recoil from abortion. Prescinding from such complicating factors as rape, incest, genetic defects, fetal defects, and the like, the main issue seems to me clear. This is the fetus' right to life. The fetus is a potential person. It is not just vegetative or animal tissue, let alone just a parasite living off the mother. Others may judge differently, but I can't get around this common-sense conviction.

All the more distressing to me, therefore, are feminist

surveys of abortion literature that ignore this central issue and common-sense conviction in order to analyze antiabortion sentiments an part of patriarchy's effort to control women.[14] Valid as such an analysis may be, it does not go to the heart of the matter, as my ecology sees things. So, I would like the coalition of feminists and Christians distressed by abortion to increase its efforts to provide alternatives: better sex education, better contraceptives, better adoption assistance, and better help for women who want to keep burdensome children.

The mystery of human life gives it an aura of sacredness, and even when one must wall the way against the simpleminded abuses, or the poetic unrealities, to which words such as "sacred" are liable, something irremovable remains. When we get callous or casual about phenomena that in a matter of months will be gurgling children, we dim the light that makes "humanity." Perhaps because they sense this, many feminists refuse to face the fetus' potential personhood. I would only ask them to be eco-logically consistent. Other feminists, who do finally believe in nothing transcendent, nothing fully sacred, are only being logical (nihilistic) when they treat abortion casually, but I hope, and suspect, that they are few.

CHRISTIAN REFLECTIONS II

Insofar as nihilism is rare, it need not concern us greatly as an ecological or political issue. However, insofar as it takes certain popular tendencies to their radical conclusion, nihilism provides faith, and perennial philosophy, an important foil. I would like to use this foil to generalize some of the lessons I have learned through ecological studies. Many have already passed in review, but I see them all now as stumbling home toward the faith with which Leonard Bernstein concludes his *Mass:* "laudate Deum"—praise God.

Annie Dillard's monstrous fecundity and the nuclear arms

race have suggested good reasons for checking our praise of God, as any other serious instances of disorder or evil could. The world is not such that a good Creator shines forth obviously, unavoidably. By the same token, however (though less noticed), there is "the problem of good." Why do the gurgling babies, the playful dolphins, the breathtaking flowers and birds stand there before us? Why *are* there such stunning somethings, when there could easily be nothing at all? Physically, aesthetically, ontologically, teleologically—in all the big-worded ways philosophers used to use—existence is a mystery. Only the Sartres of the world, those who have dimmed their eyes or twisted their souls, can deny this.

All the more, only people inexplicably dull, pusillanimous, or twisted can deny there are some good human beings, some sources of the kindness and creativity that makc life sweet. When we come close to despair over human stupidity, when the seas seem sure to turn into tar, this mystery of good offers a maternal embrace. The Earth is more than Love Canal. The Earth is also the stunning blue-and-white marvel the astronauts saw.

So, if we rightly hone a certain anger, to keep injustice on sword's point, we should also soften a certain gratitude, to keep love on heart's point. The things that exist are wonderful, even when many of them hurt us. To enjoy even a few years of life is wonderful, even when war or cancer takes life away. Both Eastern and Western religion have agreed that humanity is not the measure of things. Chuang Tzu, meditating on The Great Clod, made human time small. Like a later Chinese landscape painting, he framed human beings in the mist of eternal nature. Similarly, the biblical Christian who pondered creation with any of Tillich's metaphysical shock[15] sensed that existence is absolutely gratuitous. Before God, the sovereign font of all that is, no creature has any rights. If God chooses to strike covenants and make promises, that is God's doing. Human beings do well to remember that they are dust and unto dust they shall return. That doesn't please you, you say? Go back and think again. Does your life really make a better case against God than Job's?

These are almost simple-minded truths, largely cast aside in our sophisticated time. We can blow the world up, so surely we need not listen to old talk about creation from nothingness. But ah, my sweet, there is a difference between creation from nothingness and destruction into nothingness, isn't there? There is that little qualification that, whereas God really makes life, we really only make death. Even our gene-splicing and *in vitro* fertilization depend on prior materials God has furnished. No, we are not creators, in the profound sense. In the profound sense, we are only creatures.

I think this remains true, despite all the ignorance of it in governments, universities, literary circles, and ecclesiastical establishments. I think the praise of God, our communal *eucharistia,* remains a first obligation in truth. This does not mean I can't see the many reasons, historical and conceptual, why *eucharistia* never touches thousands of honest lips. But I venture to believe that thanksgiving is quite near to all honest hearts, whenever pain gives them the least surcease. Thanking God for the light of their eyes and the air they breathe, as the liturgical poet Huub Oosterhuis says,[16] honest people acknowledge that sunsets, children, good wine, unnecessary help, self-sacrifice, and all the other things that reflect "God" are gratuities.

So the end of my ecological reflections is near the beginning of my theological reflections: divinity, masculine and feminine, is where nature (self, society) finally points. Nothing stands there explained unless there is Everything. Pascal-like, we would not seek had we not already found: God is present heuristically, in the heart's wordless question. What sort of God? The classical God who is diffusive goodness. The process God who is persuasive, alluring love. A God of force and a God of quiet. A God of splendid *apatheia* and a God of cruciform passion. The impersonal God of Buddhism and Taoism. The lover of Hosea and Islam's Lord of the Worlds. Just about any sort of God people have decently imagined. One of my own favorites is Elijah's small, still voice. "Fear not," it says, "my hiddenness, too, serves my love."

In Fellini's film *La Strada,* a pebble triggers a revelation. In any one of our days, there is enough *there,* in the world, to trigger a revelation. Much of the revelation, if it is genuine, will boil down to the inevitable incomprehensibility of God. Much of it will suggest our reconciling ourselves to darkness, so that God's no-thing-ness may start to dawn. The very idea of "God" includes her mysterious existence, the ontological argument says. The soteriological experience, the religious person says, contains the whole in germ. We see now through a glass darkly, but then face to face. That is a hope, not a surety, and so something to bear a life's weight.

CONCLUSION: IN FRONT OF THE TITLE

In front of the titles that we give our little mental offspring lie the hopes, the fleeting glimpses, they carry forth to the wider world. Human life, it seems, depends on such hopes crucially. Frail as they are, our chosen hopes finally have to hoist our lives' weight. When the muscles have flagged, the experiences have filled many baskets, the insights have shown an infinity of possibilities, the judgments have made us skeptical, we have to decide to press ahead in hope. Of course, nature, society, and God impinge on our hopes, as do our biographies and passions. But there is something ultimate and comforting in what Aquinas called the self's capacity to return to itself. There is a homecoming, beneath the whirl of images, the clicking of the mind's cog railway, that offers us a tell-tale peace. We are made so to think on the end of things that we "come to ourselves." As Horace said, "Those who travel across the sea change the heavens, not their own minds." Significant movements such as feminism and Christianity are interested in changing minds, working conversions. When they are motivated by love, the homecoming they promote is a peace of soul, an elemental joy.

Religion sometimes gets a bad name for speaking in this oracular way. The uninitiated call it all obscurantism, self-indulgent gathering of wool. It has this danger, no doubt, but what Henri Nouwen has called "the way of the heart"[1] is so inextricably tied with the wisdom regimes of East and West that one can only oust religion and oracular speech at the price of forfeiting the sapiential quest. I sometimes think most of our culture is making this forfeit gladly, as I watch my contemporaries rush around pell-mell, outdoing one another in distraction. To find the hopes that bear a life's weight, one must pay attention.

Philip Kapleau, an American Zen roshi, tells a good story about Zen master Ikkyu:

> One day a man of the people said to Zen Master Ikkyu: "Master, will you please write for me some maxims of the highest wisdom?" Ikkyu immediately took his brush and wrote the word "Attention." "Is that all?" asked the man. "Will you not add something more?" Ikkyu then wrote twice running: "Attention. Attention." "Well," remarked the man rather irritably, "I really don't see much depth or subtlety in what you have just written." Then Ikkyu wrote the same word three times running: "Attention. Attention. Attention." Half-angered, the man demanded: "What does that word 'attention' mean anyway?" And Ikkyu answered gently: "Attention means attention."[2]

There is little spiritual life without attention.

I lean on this point because it seems to focus the prime condition for a useful colloquy between feminism and Christianity, as between any two humanisms. (Unlike many fundamentalist Christians, I do not consider "humanism" a dirty word. When Terence said, "I consider nothing human foreign to me," he spoke as an anonymous Christian. Of course, most fundamentalists admit no anonymous Christianity, but that just leaves them with a very frustrated God.) Unless the two humanisms can agree on at least some of the main lines of the human adventure; unless they can share an excitement that time just may bring understanding and justice; they are so incommensurate that conversing merely wastes their time.

But feminism and Christianity *will* begin to agree, at least to this minimal degree, if they but pay attention to the way human beings actually live. Actually, *de facto,* human beings do believe and hope and love. Actually, they do start each day as though it might justify their time and labor. Not one human being in a million is nihilistic *de facto,* so that logic and emotion join to say, really, in deed, "nothing matters." Of course something matters. Be it a child, a job, a lover, a friend, an animal, a garden or a God visited in a quiet church; some person, place, or time *matters.*

Moreover, it makes no difference that we ourselves invest these things that matter with much of their significance. Whether the significance is something we discover or something we project, it always says that the core of our selves, that quintessence best labeled our "hearts," is a lonely hunter for meaning.[3] We are all on the lookout for meaning. We are all made to find the world making sense. Camus realized this when dealing with Sisyphus. There would be no pathos in Sisyphus' labors if he did not hope to find rest at the top of the hill. There would be no sense of absurdity, no temptation to nihilism, if we did not feel drawn to meaning. As the skeptic is refuted as soon as she affirms her skepticism, so the human constitution for meaning is exercised in every intellectual probing, every desirous interpersonal encounter. What the medievals called the "transcendentals" are on our side. One, true, good, and perhaps beautiful, being prevails over nonbeing. We cannot think, act, or live as though nonbeing prevailed over being. We are not made to go out to negativity, to think disorder, to expect the surd. All of these are repugnant, not so much to our taste as to our essential build.

I am aware that, since the medievals, we have learned from the Hegelians, whose dialectics usefully show how negativities do function in a dynamic reality, somewhat as the Aristotelian potencies did. I am also aware that Eastern dialectics, such as those of Madhyamika Buddhism, move in parallel lines. None of this, I find, negates the main thesis. The main thesis is that human beings come to their time positively, working and suffering into the future through hope. Paying attention to this instinctive dynamics, fixing on the hope of the human heart from which all our theology, psychology, sociology, and ecology finally come, feminists and Christians would get their colloquy off on the right foot. From the beginning, they would see that they share an adventure spawned by life, framed by death, and illumined by symbols of immortality.[4]

THIS BOOK II

In retrospect, the most helpful way to regard the reportage and reflection of this book's four parts might be as variations on the theme of sharing a common adventure. If the adventure is to unfold its wings and move through the full range of human reality, it will perforce develop theological, psychological, sociological, and ecological dimensions. These (with the possible addition of Christology) appear to draw the main lines for an "adequate" systematics of the human adventure.[5] Assuming that the usefulness, if not the exclusivity, of such a systematic approach is clear from the foregoing eight chapters, let me now try to capture something of the personal core I find in each of the four primary areas. To put it in interrogative form, that the reader may ask in her own voice: "What are most interesting aspects of the theological, psychological, sociological, and ecological realms that this two-way reflection has uncovered?"

Theologically, I am most fascinated by the God who would really be God: living, mysterious, near as the pulse at our throats, yet ever beyond our grasp, active and effective at saving our meaning, our hopes, our selves. The more I ponder the history of religions, the more I see both great strengths and great weaknesses in the Christian conceptions of God. To be sure, one must attend carefully to the distinction between authentic and inauthentic Christianity, as we shall see in the next section. As we saw early on, the issue of a "genuine" feminism and a "genuine" Christianity, truly fit for colloquy, never leaves us very long. But prescinding from this issue, the new context of a truly world-religious dialogue casts Christian theology strictly so called in a fresh light. Many of the antagonisms theologians facilely used to set between their traditions are melting away, as more information comes in. Increasingly the suspicion arises, at least in "esoteric" personalities[6] like my own, that the religious experiences from which creative theologies arise are more complementary than contradictory.

Admittedly, in matters such as these, one's anthropological and theological assumptions play an even stronger role than in ordinary hermeneutics. Nonetheless, I find *a posteriori* evidences as well as *a priori* predilections sufficient to make me consider the Buddha, Jesus, Muhammad, Confucius, and their like more kin than strangers. So, too, with their respective versions of divinity or ultimate reality. To my mind, these different theologies make more peace than war. As a result, I find little difficulty being "large-minded" about phenomena such as the reemergence of the Goddess. Whether as a retrieval from prehistoric humanity, or as an imaginative play of the new witches, the Goddess can take a decent, defensible place in the pantheon, if we conceive "divinity" with sufficient sophistication.

Detailing such religious sophistication is a task for another book, but I can briefly indicate some of its principal components: a practical criterion of "by their fruits you will know them," with perhaps the further specification that the crucial fruits are honesty and love (considered as primitive, self-justifying experiences and concepts); an ecumenical assumption that serious people of good will who persevere in ultimate symbol-systems are finding something solid, nourishing, and of God; a discernment of spirits that stresses a balance between sober reason and emotional ecstasis, in the pattern of the Pauline balance sketched in I Corinthians 12–14; and a noetic discrimination in terms of the differentiation of consciousness, from more compact to more adequately symbolized, that allows one to delineate certain lines of historical "progress" and see the relative strengths and weaknesses of, for instance, the "cosmological myth" contrasted with the Christian doctrine of creation from nothingness.[7] The upshot for feminist theology would include a license to exploit the possibilities of the Goddess, along with a reminder that humanity has made progress since the time of agricultural religion.

Psychologically, I am most fascinated by the contemplative self that emerges through sustained prayer to the real, unco-optable God. This is the self seduced, purified, and fulfilled through the patterns of classical mysticism, such as that of John of the Cross and *The Cloud of Unknowing*. However, I am determined not to divorce this contemplative self from the eros of both mind and body, as clerical mystical theology tended to do. Creative work is also important in my psychology, especially the species we now associate with women: mothering, teaching, nursing, cooking, sewing, counseling, organizing, and the like.

Many of these creative works spill across the division between psychology and sociology, educing the political self. Indeed, pursuing the liberation of any individual, one quickly runs into "the system," which has so much to say about most people's effective liberty. Politically, I especially want to pursue the implications of Taoist dispositions, seeing whether they defuse the current madness better than Western tactics. I assume other feminists will continue with Western pressure tactics, so I'd like to develop a Taoist venture focused on emotional and atmospheric changes, as a possible contribution to stopping our winning (a few of) the battles and losing the war.

Ecologically, this Taoism suggests many of the connections necessary for feminist politics to move to science, nature, medicine, and the like. Feminism already seems well attuned to ecology, certainly better attuned than Christianity, so this may be the area where it has most to offer the colloquy. Indeed, insofar as its inner pulse is a reverence for all that exists, a feminist ecology is almost identical with a grateful theology of creation. Thus it would round the last of our corners nicely.

THE AMBIGUITIES OF CHRISTIANITY

The theology of creation is probably less central to the New Testament than the theology of salvation, and from the theology of salvation come demands to invest Christology with the full ardor of monotheism. "What was not assumed was not saved," the Fathers argued, giving some perennial status to a high, Logos Christology. Certainly one of the major tasks in the sophisticated reconception of divinity incumbent on Christians for the world-religious future is to remove the Incarnation from pejorative mythology sufficiently to allow us to hold both the oneness of the Logos Incarnate and the valuable presences of God outside Christian symbolism (for example, in sincere Goddess religion).

Anonymous Christianity is one species of solution to this problem. My impression is that anonymous Christianity has helped incline the "later" Rahner to stress Grace more than his other two "cardinal" mysteries (Trinity and Incarnation). This does not mean he has retracted the theological constructs elaborated in Christological or Trinitarian terms. It simply means that aging, deeper immersion in the pluralisms of today's global civilization, deeper appreciation of divine mystery, and the like have pushed Grace to the fore. Freely, lovingly, with a self-moving delicacy and largesse we shall never more than glimpse, God has chosen to communicate *herself*. The result is that the very horizon of human consciousness ("being") now is an offer (and successful reception) of personal divine love.

These are some of the splendid visions for which I shall never be able to repay the Christian tradition adequately. Imbibed with my mother's milk, nourished through the liturgical seasons, backed by centuries of ascetical experience, they are inseparable from my "self" and my "reality." Feeling this way, I tend to define "Christianity" in terms of such visions. They are what I find through biblical exegesis. They are what I find when I try to "think" the central phenomenon, Jesus himself. Consequently, they are my sense of "authentic" Christianity and, by that very fact, my principal equipment for detecting "inauthentic" pretenders.

From one point of view, being educated to a version of Christianity such as this is extremely freeing. As the Vatican II "Decree on Ecumenism" (#11) put it, there is a "hierarchy of truths," for some are more important than others. The dogmas from the cardinal mysteries of the Trinity, the Incarnation, and Grace are more important than the secondary dogmas of the Church or the Pope. This is not to denigrate the Church or the Pope, nor to deny one can write a systematics from the mystery of the Church, or the mystery of Revelation, or the self-authentication of Scripture. It is simply to make a firm distinction between the things of immense moment and the things of lesser moment. As long as Christianity mediates the things of immense moment—gives light, life, and love for the crux of human existence—I shall suffer no crisis in faith. Popes can come and go, churches can bicker as they will, and "Christianity" will not have fallen. If the world-view is lightsome, and some of the people are inexplicably good, Christianity will serve humanity enough to make its way.

From another point of view, this sort of education need connect only with a modest personal experience of an un-Christian institutional Church life to radicalize the graduate dramatically. Without becoming a Donatist or an anticleric, the person lured by the great vision then finds it doubly hard to take sinful or stupid pronouncements from church people as deeply binding in conscience. "For freedom Christ has set us free," Galatians 5:1 intones. Spokespersons for the Church, official or self-appointed, can counter-intone as they will, but the Spirit protects this birthright. When she serves as a second Paraclete, making that groaning prayer too deep for words where God prays to God, she frees us from all the men in funny hats, all the preachers with funny voices, who would co-opt our liberty.

To what point this rather ethereal disquisition? To the very practical point of "love and do what you will." Authentic Christianity builds up personal freedom. Without sanctioning license, it encourages people to unfold their wings, drive their minds, loosen their tongues of fire. Today I think it says to women: go to a church that honors your imaging of God. If you can't find such a church, form your own. Be patient with human weakness, never underestimate human folly, and refuse to let either take away your joy. From your centuries of marginal status, you have a special store of blessings. No one can take that store from you without chopping the beatitudes from Matthew or Luke. So be free, expecting very little and hoping everything. Join with all people who would be similarly free. Consider their sex, their color, their religion less important than their wisdom and their love. A sister bound to such a sister or brother is like a strong city. A sister talking, studying, collaborating, compassionating with such a sister or a brother is a dyad of the Kingdom. One quite adequate way of describing the Christian movement, or the feminist movement, is to call it a clustering of modules of the Kingdom. For the Kingdom is just the new, liberated existence on which all our hearts have so long been set.

Thus my authentic Christianity is the (implicit or explicit) confession of Jesus in word and deed that advances liberated human existence. It deals in justice, equal rights, fair treatment, the ministry of reconciliation, and the realization of eschatology. As some interpret Johannine theology,[8] the end-time of these things is already here. So, keeping their feet on the ground, Johannine believers labor cheerfully for better housing, cleaner rivers, fewer armaments, and more honest politics. They say we *can* have these goods, if we truly want them. God is not at all obscure on this point. The problem is our own human hearts. If we would dethrone money, power, and pride, we could have a world fit to live in. Authentic Christianity is just dethroning money, power, and pride, so as to raise up *agape*—self-spending love.

CONCORDIA II

Although the subjective journey I have traveled in this book is bound to remain somewhat obscure, for an author is never completely sure she has done more than explicate convictions she held implicitly from the outset, I now feel more confident about the concord possible between feminism and Christianity than I did when I began. Working both sides of the fence, looking at some problems from two viewpoints quite similar and at other problems from two viewpoints quite opposed, I have come to feel that "genuine" feminism and "genuine" Christianity are indeed sisterly. The honest and loving people in both camps, I am quite confident, hold many more judgments and emotions in common than they hold apart. Moreover, these people give the fringe elements in both camps a firm boot, because the fringe judgments and emotions simply don't stand up to objective reality or compassionate love. Thus, for example, I now feel calmer in opposing both radical lesbianism and right-wing Christianity than I did at the start of my surveys and reflections.

Perhaps it will help to concretize this confidence if I propose a last specimen of work in each of the four areas we have studied that I would expect both feminist and Christian readers to be able to take to heart. Two specimens come from feminist authors and two from Christian, but all four seem amenable to "cross-registration," so long as we define our allegiances carefully (in our present spirit of concord).

In my impression, Penelope Washbourn's *Becoming Woman*[9] is a feminist study of the self's development open to Christian religious insights (though the book itself is not long on them). Indeed, it makes a good beginning at the appreciative study of feminine, menstrual time we mentioned earlier. Further, Washbourn is personal in a somewhat typically feminist way, her own voice seeming to be a deliberate rejection of the pseudo-obective voice that male-dominated scholarship so regularly indulges. Consider, for example, this moving passage:

> The end of my marriage shattered my growing sense of complacency and pride at my own success. I was unmasked and that prideful girl was no more. I began to talk to friends that I had

> cut off from seeing my anguish. At first I heard only my self-pity as I told the story of the failure of my hope. Gradually the immediate grief faded and I began to rebuild. . . . Maybe nothing has been more productive of growth in myself than what I initially experienced as death (p. 74).

This is a voice trying to be honest. It speaks from a time when pain has subsided, a time when the pieces of the self have recollected, but it seems faithful to what the earlier time of torment actually was. Washbourn could deepen her insight by setting her experiences in the framework of the Christian *via negativa.* There are contemplative potentialities she seems not to plumb. But she compensates for this neglect of Christian wisdom with a personal tone, a worldly concreteness, that most Christian "psychology" sorely lacks. Consequently, I cannot see either a feminist or a Christian of good will rejecting her story, or refusing to grant that she discerns some aspects of women's life-cycle development very shrewdly. I think there would be firm accord on that.

A little more precarious, but still a good bet to win considerable accord, is the volume on women's religious lives in non-Western cultures that Nancy Falk and Rita Gross have edited recently.[10] It, too, is more feminist than Christian, but the religious lives it describes so often are manifestly full of grace that only the most hidebound Christian could fail to confess the presence of the Holy Spirit in them. I'm not sure that Falk and Gross would be overjoyed by this confession, but some of their book's subjects, such as Ma Jnanananda of Madras, surely would. Ma Jnanananda is a holy woman in the tradition of Advaita Vedanta Hinduism, whose predilection is to see the one Brahman everywhere. Such Hindus are "ecumenical" almost to a fault, and they seldom feel constrained by definitional barriers the way Western academics do. Consequently, they would be proud to be described as full of (Christian) grace.

My two Christian candidates for eliciting accord or concord pertain to the social and ecological realms. Marie

Augusta Neal's *A Socio-Theology of Letting Go*[11] meditates movingly on the transfers of wealth and power necessary if anything approaching worldwide social justice is to emerge. Its analogous application to sexual injustices should be clear, and it will only offend those feminists (or Christians) who cannot bear reminders of the prophetic tradition. Thus Neal will be no friend to feminists who think their movement is mainly "getting a piece of the action," but deeper types, willing to move below the materialist good life in search of more profound commonweal, will find much in it to approve. Like the Greek tragedians and the New Testament evangelists, Neal knows that certain ways of saving one's life are losing it, while certain ways of losing one's life are saving it. I hope more and more Christians and feminists will come together in this knowledge.

Last, I find a Christian ecology that many feminists could approve in the following lines from a recent ascetical theology:

> Nature inculcates a twofold holism. Biologically, as a structure of physical life, we are immersed in something organic, something weblike and social. Psychologically, we have at least the potentiality for an ecstatic appreciation of this—for a wonderful mutuality with otters and beavers. Therefore, those who deal only with discrete phenomena miss something crucial in both nature and themselves. Therefore, reductionist methods that isolate parts need the complement of contemplative methods that appreciate the whole. Our culture is pervaded with reductionism, so most of us need special prodding to go out in delight at a living whole. Perhaps the ecological movement's greatest significance, spiritually, will be to increase our ability to do this.[12]

Having written this book largely in the hope that it might increase the delight of some feminists and some Christians by showing them how they might join in a greater living whole, I find this a good place to conclude. May we all keep going, however, so that, feminists and Christians, we find Concordia a good place to celebrate the tricentennial.

NOTES

INTRODUCTION: BEHIND THE TITLE

1. Karl Rahner, "The One Christ and the Universality of Salvation," *Theological Investigations,* XVI (New York: Seabury Press, 1979), p. 219.
2. See Bernard Lonergan, *Method in Theology* (New York: Herder and Herder, 1972), p. 105.
3. Wilfred Cantwell Smith, *Toward a World Theology* (Philadelphia: Westminster Press, 1981), p. 189.
4. See Eloise C. Snyder, ed., *The Study of Women* (New York: Harper & Row, 1979). My chapter is on pp. 267-95.
5. Eric Voegelin, *From Enlightenment to Revolution* (Durham, N.C.: Duke University Press, 1975), pp. 240-302.
6. Jerry Falwell, *Listen, America!* (Garden City, N.Y.: Doubleday, 1980), p. 151.
7. *Ibid.,* p. 13.
8. *Ibid.,* p. 152.
9. Denise Lardner Carmody, *Women and World Religions* (Nashville: Abingdon, 1979).
10. See *International Bulletin of Missionary Research,* 5/2 (April 1981), p. 92.
11. Smith, *ibid.,* p. 193.
12. See Jon Sobrino, *Christology at the Crossroads* (Maryknoll, N.Y.: Orbis, 1978).

CHAPTER ONE: THE NEW FOCUS ON THE GODDESS

1. See, for example, Phyllis Trible, *God and the Rhetoric of Sexuality* (Philadelphia: Fortress Press, 1978).
2. Gael Hodgkins, "Sedna: Images of the Transcendent in an Eskimo Goddess," *Beyond Androcentrism,* Rita M. Gross, ed. (Missoula, Mont.: Scholars Press, 1977), pp. 305-14.
3. See Eric Voegelin, *Order and History,* IV (Baton Rouge: Louisiana State University Press, 1974), pp. 7-11.

4. Rita M. Gross, "Hindu Female Deities as a Resource for the Contemporary Recovery of the Goddess," *Journal of the American Academy of Religion,* XLVI/3 (September 1978), pp. 269-91.

5. Joanna Rogers Macy, "Perfection of Wisdom : Mother of All Buddhas," *Beyond Androcentrism,* p. 316.

6. See C. N. Tay, "Kuan-yin: The Cult of Half Asia," *History of Religions,* 16/2 (November 1976), pp. 147-77.

7. Carol P. Christ, "Why Women Need the Goddess," *Womanspirit Rising,* Carol P. Christ and Judith Plaskow, eds. (San Francisco: Harper & Row, 1979), p. 273. The quotation is from Ntosake Shange's *For Colored Girls Who Have Considered Suicide When the Rainbow Is Enuf* and occurs at the very end of the play.

8. Simone de Beauvoir, *The Second Sex* (New York: Vintage, 1974), p. 691.

9. Starhawk (Miriam Simos), *The Spiral Dance* (San Francisco: Harper & Row, 1979).

10. Ernest Callenbach, *Ecotopia* (New York: Bantam, 1975).

11. In addition to Christ and Starhawk, see Naomi Goldenberg, *Changing of the Gods* (Boston: Beacon Press, 1979).

12. See, for instance, Edward Schillebeeckx, *Interim Report on the Books Jesus & Christ* (New York: Seabury Press, 1981).

13. Irenaeus, *Adversus Haereses,* IV, 20, 7.

14. This is Karl Rahner's core Christology. See his *Foundations of Christian Faith* (New York: Seabury Press, 1978).

15. Schillebeeckx, *Interim Report,* p. 52.

16. Bernard Lonergan, *De Verbo Incarnato* (Rome: Gregorian University Press, 1964), thesis 17.

17. My positions on the world religions are available in Denise Lardner Carmody and John Tully Carmody, *Ways to the Center: An Introduction to World Religions* (Belmont, Calif.: Wadsworth, 1981).

18. My main debt here is to Eric Voegelin. See, for instance, his recent *Conversations with Eric Voegelin* (Montreal: Thomas More, 1980), or his *Anamnesis* (Notre Dame, Ind.: University of Notre Dame Press, 1978).

19. Paula Fredriksen Landes makes an equivalent point in her review of several recent feminist works. See *Signs* 6/2 (Winter, 1980), pp. 328-34.

20. The term comes from Raimundo Panikkar, *The Trinity and the Religious Experience of Man* (Maryknoll, N.Y.: Orbis, 1973), e.g., p. 16, who means that human corporeality assures we will worship God through material objects carrying something of the divine allure.

CHAPTER TWO: THE NEW FOCUS ON JESUS

1. Samuel Terrien, *The Elusive Presence: Toward a New Biblical Theology* (New York: Harper & Row, 1978).

2. Perhaps my *What Are They Saying About Non-Christian Faith?* (Ramsey, N.J.: Paulist, 1982) would be useful at this point.

3. Edward Schillebeeckx, *Interim Report on the Books Jesus & Christ* (New York: Crossroad, 1981), p. 56.

4. Paul Ricoeur, "The Logic of Jesus, the Logic of God," *Christianity and Crisis,* 39/20 (December 24, 1979), pp. 324-27.

5. On the cross-attribution of divine and human properties, see "Communicatio Idiomatum," Karl Rahner and Herbert Vorgrimler, *Theological Dictionary* (New York: Herder & Herder, 1965), p. 90.

6. See José Miranda, *Marx and the Bible* (Maryknoll, N.Y.: Orbis, 1974).

7. William M. Thompson, *Jesus, Lord and Savior: A Theopathic Christology* (New York: Paulist Press, 1980).

8. Langdon Gilkey, *Message and Existence: An Introduction to Christian Theology* (New York: Seabury Press, 1979).

9. Edward Schillebeeckx, *Christ: The Experience of Jesus as Lord* (New York: Seabury Press, 1980), pp. 512-14.

10. Lucas Grollenberg, *Jesus* (Philadelphia: Westminster Press, 1978).

11. Judith Plaskow, *Sex, Sin and Grace: Women's Experience and the Theologies of Reinhold Niebuhr and Paul Tillich* (Lanham, Md.: University Press of America, 1980).

12. See Valerie Saiving Goldstein, "The Human Situation: A Feminine View," *Journal of Religion,* 40 (1960), p. 108. Plaskow quotes this on p. 1. The article is reprinted in *Womanspirit Rising,* Carol P. Christ and Judith Plaskow, eds. (San Francisco: Harper & Row, 1979), pp. 25-42. My own phenomenology of the issue is sketched in Denise Lardner Carmody and John Tully Carmody, "Females, Males, and Religion," *Religion in Life,* XLVII (1978), pp. 190-96.

13. Note, as a helpful model, Robert McAfee Brown's change of Gustavo Gutierrez's sexist language in Robert McAfee Brown, *Gustavo Gutierrez* (Atlanta: John Knox Press, 1980).

14. *America,* 144/13 (April 4, 1981), p. 283, in review of John Tully Carmody and Denise Lardner Carmody, *Contemporary Catholic Theology* (San Francisco: Harper & Row, 1980).

15. Rosemary Radford Ruether, "A Religion for Women: Sources and Strategies," *Christianity and Crisis,* 39/19 (December 10, 1979), p. 308.

16. Dorothee Sölle, "More on God-Talk," *Christianity and Crisis,* 41/10 (June 8, 1981), p. 169.

17. See Vladimir Lossky, *The Mystical Theology of the Eastern Church* (Crestwood, N.Y.: SVS Press, 1976).

18. See Michael Buckley, "Atheism and Contemplation," *Theological Studies,* 40/4 (December 1979), pp. 680-94.

CHAPTER THREE: THE FEMINIST SELF

1. Carolyn Wood Sherif, "What Every Intelligent Person Should Know About Psychology and Women," *The Study of Women: Enlarging Perspectives of Social Reality,* Eloise C. Synder, ed. (New York: Harper & Row, 1979), pp. 143-83.

2. Dorothy Dinnerstein, *The Mermaid and the Minotaur* (New York: Harper & Row, 1976).

3. One thinks of Erik Erikson's correlation of the "Madonna" visage with the first epigenetic virtue of hope. A good feminist overview of psychoanalytic theories such as Erikson's is *Women & Analysis,* Jean Strouse, ed. (New York: Grossman, 1974).

4. As counterbalance to *The Mermaid and the Minotaur,* see Robert Coles and Jane Hallowell Coles, *Women of Crisis* (New York: Delta, 1978). The Coleses put qualifications on Dinnerstein's accuracy regarding mothers' (especially working-class mothers') angry desire for less time with their children. See p. 289, in the excellent bibliography.

5. Carol P. Christ, *Diving Deep and Surfacing: Women Writers on Spiritual Quest* (Boston: Beacon Press, 1980). My comments in this section draw upon my review in *Religion in Life,* XLIX/4 (Winter 1980), pp. 507-509.

6. For further exploration of black women's experience, see Michelle Wallace, *Black Macho & the Myth of the Super-Woman* (New York: Warner Books, 1979). Several black Christian perspectives are available in Gayraud S. Wilmore and James H. Cone, eds., *Black Theology: A Documentary History* (Maryknoll, N.Y.: Orbis, 1979).

7. Margaret Atwood, *Life Before Man* (New York: Simon and Schuster, 1979).

8. Doris Lessing, *Canopus in Argos: Archives, 1: Shikasta* (New York: Knopf, 1979); *2: The Marriages Between Zones Three, Four, and Five* (New York: Knopf, 1980); *3: The Sirian Experiments* (New York: Knopf, 1981). I attempted a correlation of the early Lessing (specifically, the Lessing of *The Golden Notebook*) with Christian theology in my article, "Feminist Redemption: Doris Lessing and Bernard Lonergan," *Andover Newton Quarterly,* 16/2 (November 1975), pp. 119-30. The later Lessing seems to me a writer of immense vision, so I find stylistic strictures such as Joan Didion's in *The White Album* (New York: Simon & Schuster, 1979, pp. 119-25) almost petty. It is true that Didion's criticism focuses on work prior to *Canopus in Argos.* However, Lessing's style has not improved in the meantime, nor has her concern for art, in Didion's craft-stressing sense, increased. Perhaps Didion's own elegant style betrays the psychological roots of her objections. Unable to create anything approaching Lessing's work in positive stature, she settles for surgical (incisive, destructive) precision.

9. Madonna Kolbenschlag, *Kiss Sleeping Beauty Good-Bye* (Garden City, N.Y.: Doubleday, 1979).

10. Gail Sheehy, *Passages: Predictable Crises of Adult Life* (New York: E. P. Dutton, 1974), pp. 293-94.

11. See Erik Erikson, "Erikson on Erikson," *Women & Analysis*, pp. 291-340.

12. See Jacob Neusner, "Thematic or Systematic Description: The Case of Mishnah's Division of Women," *Method and Meaning in Ancient Judaism* (Missoula, Mont.: Scholars Press, 1979).

13. Erik H. Erikson, "Dr. Borg's Life-Cycle," *Daedalus*, 105/2 (Spring 1976), p. 23.

14. On Christian adulthood, see Evelyn Whitehead and James Whitehead, *Christian Life Patterns* (Garden City, N.Y.: Doubleday, 1979).

CHAPTER FOUR: CHRISTIAN SELFHOOD

1. Rosemary Ruether and Eleanor McLaughlin, eds., *Women of Spirit* (New York: Simon & Schuster, 1979).

2. See Joann Wolski Conn, "Women's Spirituality: Restriction and Reconstruction," *Cross Currents*, XXX/3 (Fall 1980), pp. 293-308.

3. Robert Coles and Jane Hallowell Coles, *Women of Crisis: Lives of Struggle and Hope* (New York: Delta, 1978).

4. Robert Coles, *The Children of Crisis, V: Privileged Ones* (Boston: Little, Brown, 1977).

5. See, for example, Lawrence Cunningham, *The Meaning of Saints* (San Francisco: Harper & Row, 1980), pp. 151-53.

6. See William Johnston, *The Inner Eye of Love* (San Francisco: Harper & Row, 1978).

7. See Sergius Bolshakof and M. Basil Pennington, *In Search of True Wisdom* (Garden City, N.Y.: Doubleday, 1979), p. 168.

8. Note, for example, the theoretical poverty of *Women and the Workplace*, Martha Blaxall and Barbara Reagan, eds. (Chicago: University of Chicago Press, 1976).

9. Studs Terkel, *Working* (New York: Pantheon, 1974), p. xxiv.

10. Philip Kapleau, *Zen: Dawn in the West* (Garden City, N.Y.: Doubleday, 1980), p. 12.

11. See Thomas Merton, *The Way of Chuang Tzu* (New York: New Directions, 1965), pp. 45-47.

12. See Michael Polanyi, *Personal Knowledge* (New York: Harper Torchbooks, 1964), pp. 49-65.

13. E. F. Schumacher, *Small Is Beautiful: Economics As If People Mattered* (New York: Harper & Row, 1973), p. 51.

14. E. F. Schumacher, *Good Work* (New York: Harper & Row, 1979), p. 138.

15. Mary Gordon, *The Company of Women* (New York: Random House, 1980).

16. Mary Daly, *Gyn/Ecology: The Metaethics of Radical Feminism* (Boston: Beacon Press, 1978).

17. Among the many solid historical treatments, see Rosemary Ruether, ed., *Religion and Sexism* (New York: Simon & Schuster, 1974); Elizabeth Clark and Herbert Richardson, eds., *Women and Religion: A Sourcebook of Christian Thought* (New York: Harper & Row, 1977); George Tavard, *Woman in Christian Tradition* (Notre Dame, Ind.: University of Notre Dame Press, 1973).

18. Naomi R. Goldenberg, *Changing of the Gods* (Boston: Beacon Press, 1979), p. 5.

CHAPTER FIVE: CHRISTIAN SOCIAL THEORY

1. Rosemary R. Ruether, "Why Socialism Needs Feminism, & Vice Versa," *Christianity and Crisis,* 40/7 (April 28, 1980), pp. 103-108.

2. See Eric Voegelin, *From Enlightenment to Revolution* (Durham, N.C.: Duke University Press, 1975), and Igor Shafarevich, *The Socialist Phenomenon* (New York: Harper & Row, 1980).

3. See Ernesto Cardenal, *The Gospel in Solentiname,* 3 vols. (Maryknoll, N.Y.: Orbis, 1978, 1979, 1979).

4. See Sergio Torres and John Eagleson, eds., *The Challenge of Basic Christian Communities* (Maryknoll, N.Y.: Orbis, 1981).

5. Penny Lernoux, *Cry of the People* (Garden City, N.Y.: Doubleday, 1980).

6. See Cora Ferro, "The Latin American Woman: The Praxis and Theology of Liberation," *The Challenge of Basic Christian Communities,* pp. 24-37.

7. *The Gospel in Solentiname,* vol. 3, pp. 70-71.

8. See Leonardo Boff, "Theological Characteristics of a Grass-Roots Church," *The Challenge of Basic Christian Communities,* pp. 124-44.

9. See Kofi Appiah-Kubi and Sergio Torres, eds., *African Theology en Route* (Maryknoll, N.Y.: Orbis, 1979).

10. Patricia Park, "Women and Liturgy," *Women Ministers,* Judith L. Weidman, ed. (San Francisco: Harper & Row, 1981), pp. 78-79.

11. Adrienne Rich, "Disloyal to Civilization: Feminism, Racism, Gynephobia," *On Lies, Secrets, and Silence* (New York: W. W. Norton, 1979), pp. 275-310.

12. Ross S. Kraemer, review of *Gyn/Ecology, Signs,* 5/2 (Winter 1979), pp. 354-56.

13. Elaine Pagels, *The Gnostic Gospels* (New York: Random House, 1979), especially pp. 48-69.

CHAPTER SIX: FEMINIST POLITICAL THEORY

1. Dolores Hayden, "What Would a Non-Sexist City Be Like? Speculations on Housing, Urban Design, and Human Work," *Signs,* 5/3 Supplement (Spring 1980), S170-87.

2. Peggy Reeves Sanday, *Female Power and Male Dominance: On the Origins of Sexual Inequality* (Cambridge: Cambridge University Press, 1981), pp. 113-14.

3. See, for example, Margery Wolf, "Chinese Women: Old Skills in a New Context," *Woman, Culture & Society,* M. Z. Rosaldo and L. Lamphere, eds. (Stanford, Calif.: Stanford University Press, 1974), pp. 157-72; Samuel C. Heilman, *Synagogue Life* (Chicago: University of Chicago Press, 1976).

4. Sanday, *Female Power and Male Dominance,* p. 115.

5. *Ibid.,* p. 125.

6. Jane Fishburne Collier, "Women in Politics," *Woman, Culture & Society,* pp. 89-96.

7. Elise Boulding, *Women in the Twentieth Century World* (New York: Sage Publications, 1977). As further background, see her *The Underside of History: A View of Women Through Time* (Boulder, Colo.: Westview Press, 1976).

8. Alison Jaggar, "Political Philosophies of Women's Liberation," *Philosophy and Women,* Sharon Bishop and Marjorie Weinzweig, eds. (Belmont, Calif.: Wadsworth, 1979), pp. 258-65.

9. See Huston Smith, *Forgotten Truth: The Primordial Tradition* (New York: Harper & Row, 1976), and E. F. Schumacher, *A Guide for the Perplexed* (New York: Harper & Row, 1977).

10. Eric Voegelin, *Conversations with Eric Voegelin* (Montreal: Thomas More Institute, 1980), p. 100.

11. Two good general works of Christian feminist politics are Mary P. Burke, *Reaching for Justice* (Washington, D.C.: Center of Concern, 1980), and Letty M. Russell, *The Future of Partnership* (Philadelphia: Westminster Press, 1979).

CHAPTER SEVEN: CHRISTIAN THEOLOGY OF NATURE

1. For general background, see David Spring and Eileen Spring, eds., *Ecology and Religion in History* (New York: Harper & Row, 1974).

2. Robert Coles, *The Old Ones of New Mexico* (Albuquerque: University of New Mexico Press, 1973), p. 6.

3. See Ellen Marie Chen, "Tao as the Great Mother and the Influence of Motherly Love in the Shaping of Chinese Philosophy," *History of Religions,* 14/1 (1974), pp. 51-63.

4. Denise Lardner Carmody, "Taoist Reflections on Feminism," *Religion in Life,* 44 (1977), pp. 234-44.

5. Lester C. Thurow, *The Zero-Sum Society* (New York: Penguin Books, 1981), p. 105.

6. Herman E. Daly, "The Ecological and Moral Necessity for Limiting Economic Growth," *Faith and Science in an Unjust World,* vol. I, ed. Roger L. Shinn (Philadelphia: Fortress Press, 1980), pp. 212-20.

7. See, for instance, C. T. Kurien, "A Third World Perspective," *Faith and Science in an Unjust World,* pp. 220-25.

8. Karen Lebacqz, "Bio-ethics: Some Challenges from a Liberation Perspective," *Faith and Science in an Unjust World,* pp. 272-81.

9. John B. Cobb, Jr., Review of Andrew Linzey, *Animal Rights, Environmental Ethics,* 2/1 (Spring 1980), p. 89.

10. See John Carmody, "A Note on the God-World Relation in Whitehead's *Process and Reality,*" *Philosophy Today,* 15/4 (Winter 1971), pp. 302-12.

11. John B. Cobb, Jr. and David Ray Griffin, *Process Theology: An Introductory Exposition* (Philadelphia: Westminster Press, 1976), p. 155.

12. See also Cobb's *Is It Too Late?: A Theology of Ecology* (Beverly Hills, Calif.: Bruce, 1971); and Ian Barbour, ed., *Earth Might Be Fair* (Englewood Cliffs, N.J.: Prentice-Hall, 1972).

13. Annie Dillard, *Pilgrim at Tinker Creek* (New York: Harper's Magazine Press, 1974); and Lewis Thomas, *The Lives of a Cell* (New York: Viking, 1974).

14. See Ernest Callenbach, *Ecotopia* (New York: Bantam, 1977).

15. Ian G. Barbour, ed., *Finite Resources and the Human Future* (Minneapolis: Augsburg, 1976).

16. Nicholas Georgescu-Roegen, "The Entropy Law and the Economic Problem," *Toward a Steady-State Economy,* Herman E. Daly, ed., (San Francisco: W. H. Freeman, 1973), pp. 46-47.

17. See Carl Djerassi, *The Politics of Contraception,* vol. I (Stanford, Calif.: The Portable Stanford, 1979), p. 10.

18. Barbara Ward, *Progress for a Small Planet* (New York: W. W. Norton, 1979).

CHAPTER EIGHT: FEMINIST THEORY OF NATURE

1. Doris Lessing, *Canopus in Argos: Archives, Vol. I: Shikasta* (New York: Knopf, 1979).

2. C. G. Jung, *Memories, Dreams, Reflections* (New York: Vintage, 1973), pp. 250-51.

3. Susan Griffin, *Woman and Nature* (New York: Harper & Row, 1978).

4. Sherry B. Ortner, "Is Female to Male As Nature Is to Culture?"

Woman, Culture & Society, M. Z. Rosaldo and L. Lamphere, eds. (Stanford, Calif.: Stanford University Press, 1974), pp. 67-88.

5. See Carol MacCormack and Marilyn Strathern, eds., *Nature, Culture and Gender* (Cambridge: Cambridge University Press, 1980).

6. See William LaFleur, "Saigyo and the Buddhist Value of Nature," *History of Religions,* 13 (1973-1974), pp. 93-128, 227-48.

7. See Margaret Mead, *Sex and Temperament* (New York: William Morrow, 1963); and *Male & Female* (New York: William Morrow, 1975).

8. Annie Dillard, *Pilgrim at Tinker Creek* (New York: Harper's Magazine Press, 1974).

9. See Lao Tzu, *Tao Te Ching,* chapter 5.

10. Helen Caldicott, *Nuclear Madness* (Brookline, Mass.: Autumn Press, 1978).

11. Carl Djerassi, *The Politics of Contraception,* vol. I (Stanford, Calif.: The Portable Stanford, 1979), p. 23.

12. *Ibid.,* p. 30.

13. See Carl N. Degler, *At Odds: Women and the Family in America from the Revolution to the Present* (Oxford: Oxford University Press, 1980), p. 228.

14. See Barbara Hayler, "Abortion," *Signs,* 5/2 (Winter 1979), pp. 307-23.

15. See Paul Tillich, *Systematic Theology,* vol. I (Chicago: University of Chicago Press, 1967), pp. 163-68.

16. Huub Oosterhuis, *Your Word Is Near* (New York: Newman Press, 1968), p. 114.

CONCLUSION: IN FRONT OF THE TITLE

1. Henri Nouwen, *The Way of the Heart* (New York: Seabury Press, 1980).

2. Philip Kapleau, *The Three Pillars of Zen* (Boston: Beacon, 1967), pp. 10-11.

3. See Michael Polanyi and Harry Prosch, *Meaning* (Chicago: University of Chicago Press, 1975).

4. See Eric Voegelin, "Immortality: Experience and Symbol," *Harvard Theological Review,* LX (1967), 235-79; and "The Gospel and Culture," *Jesus and Man's Hope,* eds. D. Miller and D. Hadidian (Pittsburgh: Pittsburgh Theological Seminary, 1971), pp. 59-101.

5. See John Carmody, *Theology for the 1980s* (Philadelphia: Westminster Press, 1980).

6. See Huston Smith, "Frithjof Schuon's *The Transcendent Unity of Religion: Pro,*" *Journal of the American Academy of Religion,* XLIV (1976), pp. 715-19.

7. See John Carmody, "Voegelin's Noetic Differentiation: Religious Implications," *Horizons,* 8 (1981), pp. 223-46.

8. See, for example, José Miranda, *Being and the Messiah* (Maryknoll, N.Y.: Orbis, 1977).

9. Penelope Washbourn, *Becoming Woman* (New York: Harper & Row, 1977).

10. Nancy A. Falk and Rita M. Gross, eds., *Unspoken Worlds: Women's Lives in Non-Western Cultures* (San Francisco: Harper & Row, 1980).

11. Marie Augusta Neal, *A Socio-Theology of Letting Go: The Role of a First World Church Facing Third World Peoples* (New York: Paulist Press, 1977).

12. John Carmody, *The Progressive Pilgrim* (Notre Dame, Ind. Fides/Claretian, 1980), p. 26.

INDEX